The Savvy Manager

5 Skills That Drive Optimal Performance

Jane R. Flagello and Sandra Bernard Dugas

ASTD
PRESS

Alexandria, Virginia

© 2009 the American Society for Training & Development

ASTD Press is an internationally renowned source of insightful and practical information on workplace learning and performance topics, including training basics, evaluation and return on investment, instructional systems development, e-learning, leadership, and career development.

Ordering information: Books published by ASTD Press can be purchased by visiting our website at store.astd.org or by calling 800.628.2783 or 703.683.8100.

Library of Congress Control Number: 2007939863

ISBN-10: 1-56286-532-3
ISBN-13: 978-1-56286-532-0

ASTD Press Editorial Staff:

Director: Cat Russo
Manager, Acquisitions and Author Relations: Mark Morrow
Editorial Manager: Jacqueline Edlund-Braun
Senior Associate Editor: Tora Estep
Associate Editor: Maureen Soyars

Copyeditor: Alfred Imhoff
Indexer: April Davis
Proofreader: Kris Patenaude
Interior Design and Production: Kathleen Schaner
Cover Design: Ana Ilieva

Printed by Victor Graphics, Inc., Baltimore, MD, www.victorgraphics.com

Contents

Foundations of the Savvy Manager

One resists the invasion of armies, but not an idea whose time has come.
—Victor Hugo

This is not the business world of our fathers! Today's business world is global, where competing successfully intensifies the need for fundamental changes in how you manage. Doing "more with less" and "lean and mean" gives way to realistic strategies. It demands that you work smarter, not harder. And today, smarter means more than just *doing* things differently. You must *think* differently! Your thoughts ground your actions. As your thoughts shift, new actions that are more sustainable emerge from a deeper understanding of what's happening.

The simple truth is that achieving consistent high performance is all about the relationship between people and work. Sustainable change comes from an integrated perspective of employees as people and work as an expression of service. Performance explodes as organizations reinvent themselves with fresh ideas about how to engage people, promote communication, engender trust, inspire purpose, and empower action. Harnessing the creativity and productivity of all employees in concrete ways generates prosperity for all. Employees are seen as vital assets in the performance and profitability equation.

Fundamental change is the focus of the book you now hold in your hands. You are about to work with two highly accomplished, master coaches. Our underlying goal is to change behavior: your behavior. Your coaching will center on optimizing your managerial and leadership competencies by incorporating five new skills that enable your best performance. The five skills of self-managing, reflecting, acting consciously, collaborating, and evolving drive optimal performance and shape the savvy manager within you. Understand now—*managing with savvy* is all about you!

The Craft of the Manager

One could say that management is the identification, alignment, and integration of available and appropriate resources, in just the right mix, to achieve a desired outcome. It is a discipline steeped in the operational science of precision, processes, and execution: Input leads to transformation, which leads to output. Systems, quantitative measurements, schedules, and processes monitor and control the critical balance between inputs and outputs to ensure the company achieves intended results. Procedures direct people and processes to perform efficiently and effectively. At first glance, this might seem effortless, with management appearing to be "common sense" or just the job of establishing and following a plan. Managing time, analyzing systems, balancing budgets, and allocating resources are all part of the "black-and-white," scientific part of management. These powerful tools are critical, but insufficient alone to manage today.

> *What is really essential is this: every form of life is interrelated. We are trapped in an inescapable network of mutuality, bound by a common destiny. Whatever affects us directly, affects everybody indirectly.*
>
> —Martin Luther King Jr.

The actual task of managing processes with flawless precision rests on the shoulders of people, who are both complicated and unique. Organizations, as a collection of people engaged in work, make managing more about "art" than science. Here is where most managers find themselves unsure and struggling. The savvy manager we are coaching you to become develops that unique ability to work with the human dimension of his or her company—with each individual person, both separately and together. If you have been fortunate enough to work with or for a savvy manager, you know firsthand the distinction being made here. You can also appreciate the challenge!

Drucker Frames the Way

Throughout his illustrious career, Peter F. Drucker, one of the greatest management intellects of our time, held that management had three primary functions: managing the business, utilizing the full complement of available resources, and effectively matching employees with the work required. In his later years, he added an all encompassing social responsibility function to the list (Drucker 1954).

Using Drucker's functions as a starting point, we integrate new thinking perspectives required for you to effectively manage today. As you review table P-1, think about your own actions and thoughts. Pay particular attention to the *savvy translations* as these come from our coaching voices and speak to your development. It is here that you will find new challenges to master as you develop your basic managerial expertise. Consider these three questions:

- Are your management skills producing the results you want?
- What are your greatest challenges and opportunities?
- Where do you want to grow?

Table P-1. Functions of Managers

Function	Standard Description	Savvy Translation
Manage the business	Managers are tasked with creating the appropriate set of circumstances to achieve profitable business performance.	You need to *think like an owner*. You must envision the "big picture" of your organization and its long-term global fit. Only then can you analyze current processes and systems, aligning these with employees' capabilities. The savvy challenge focuses on your ability to achieve profitability now and taking the steps necessary to be profitable tomorrow.
Make all resources productive	Managers blend together and make the various resources available to the business productive. Efficiency, choosing wisely, and decisive actions direct this function.	You must *choose wisely*. Resources are costly. Savvy managers assess their needs and the available resources in ways that enable them to select only the best. These are the resources most suitable to the tasks at hand and the resources that show promise for future possibilities.
Manage workers and the work	The manager must align available resources, employee skills, and the work flow to optimize results. When humans enter the picture, "the many shades of gray" appear. Clearly, maximizing process and systems with people presents the greatest challenge.	You need to *become the conductor*. You must channel all your actions toward engaging your human resources—the people who do the work. By connecting with the full person (heart, mind, and spirit), you bring out the best in each player, aligning that "best" to continuously produce outstanding results.
Support social responsibility	Managing the business in ways that sustain the means for people to earn a living and create a life for themselves, their families, and their communities supports organizational social responsibility.	You represent the *quality of life gatekeeper*. The challenges of daily life are ameliorated when people have meaningful work and can get their own and their family's needs met.

Source: Adapted from Drucker (1954).

An Inside-Out Approach

Building mastery of your managerial art requires that you first examine your own thoughts and actions. You must intentionally step out of your comfort zone and attempt new behaviors that will feel uncomfortable at first. Next, examine how your actions enhance your ability to motivate yourself and inspire your people to perform at the highest levels. It all comes down to this simple truth: If you want your organization to be better, the first step is for you to *manage* better. The challenge we place before you, and the one to which you must fully commit, is your own learning. Our approach is all about you learning more about yourself. It is what Timothy Gallwey (2000) calls the "inner game." Your savvy skills are there, ready for you to utilize. You'll need to awaken them, sharpen them with practice, and let them direct your actions. Start now. Get a notebook or journal and capture all the thoughts that spring to mind as you are reading. Our coaching throughout the pages that follow can enhance your learning and transform you into a more highly effective, *savvy* manager.

> *People work for a paycheck.... But if that's the only reason they can find for going to work every day, they won't work with the imagination, the resourcefulness, the steady willingness, and the sensitivity to the marketplace that we've got to promote all the way through the organization if we want to prevail in today's environment.*
>
> —James Champy

The book includes nine chapters, each of which focuses on a traditional management topic seen as indispensable for our time. Every chapter includes a "Real Time" story, a compilation of actual situations faced by our coaching clients with identifying details altered to protect privacy and confidentiality. The five savvy skills are introduced in chapter 1, and these skills are then woven into each succeeding chapter enabling you to build your competencies. Throughout the chapters, pay particular attention to the "Savvy Translations," which distill the major points of the chapter into bite-sized nuggets to help you remember and apply what you have learned.

Each chapter concludes with a section called "The Bottom Line" that summarizes key concepts and coaches you to take the steps needed to succeed. To further coach you to action, we have included a "Use It or Lose It" subsection intended to help you reflect on what you "got" from the chapter. To increase your ability to think in more expansive ways, a "Reflection Interval" subsection follows. The vignette—story, parable, or poem—we have included here challenges you to think about the topic of the chapter in new, creative ways. The "Coaching for Action: Driving Optimal Performance" subsection provides specific exercises for practicing new skills and behaviors to build your savvy. You can increase your learning when you invest the time and effort to complete these activities.

More on the Web

Beginning with chapter 2, you will find a "Lagniappe" subsection at the end of each chapter. Giving lagniappe (pronounced lan-yap) is the common French Acadian practice of offering a little something extra, which we are doing here. You will be directed to additional skill-building worksheets and exercises online at www.astd.org/SavvyManager. The page also contains a Learning Annex that includes general management concepts and theories, which we link to learning in selected chapters. Bookmark the book's companion website, www.thesavvymanager.biz, and visit us frequently for updates and additional learning.

The Bottom Line: Finding Your Savvy

"Savvy" is an inside job. These new skills require practice. Take the learning introduced in the pages that follow and apply it to your everyday life. You will learn to accept that you can't change another person—you can only change yourself. As you become more insightful and internally focused, you will grow and develop your full potential for success. The five-step process given in table P-2 will help you integrate your learning from the coaching we are offering. Use it as you build your managerial savvy!

Table P-2. The Five-Step Savvy Management Process

Step	Description
Set learning goals	Set learning goals for yourself and assign realistic deadlines to meet these goals. Look at each chapter or lagniappe title and ask yourself, *What do I want to learn about this topic?* Write down your answer and keep it in front of you as you read the material. The most successful managers are those who set learning goals on a daily basis.
Share your learning	Sharing what you learn with others deepens your understanding. When you teach something to another person, your learning becomes twice as powerful. Discuss what you read with co-workers, family, and friends. Find a learning partner with whom you can discuss new concepts.
Practice	Practice what you read and learn in each chapter. Experiment with techniques and strategies that incorporate concepts into your work environment. Use the activities at the end of each chapter to build your competence and expand your confidence using new concepts.
Reflect	Make time for reflection. Complex business issues require deeper examination. Reflection increases awareness, informing your choices and allowing you to make decisions that are responsive, not reactionary. Utilize your senses to connect with both your head and heart. *What could you have done differently to get a result closer to the one you really wanted?*
Measure progress	Measure your results against quantified goals. Attach what you learn to measurable outcomes in your organization over which you have authority and influence. Set up criteria that support your time and effort to learn and apply new concepts from your reading. Think of it as your personal return-on-investment.

Reflection Interval

Your actions matter more than you might think. Many versions of the following story have been told and retold to make the point about how our actions matter. What fresh understanding emerges about your ability to make a difference at work from "The Starfish Story" below?

The Starfish Story

Adapted from *The Star Thrower* by Loren Eiseley (1979); the author of this version is unknown.

Once upon a time, there was an elderly man who used to go to the ocean to do his writing. He had a habit of walking on the beach before he began his work. One day, as he was walking along the shore, he looked down the beach and saw a human figure moving like a dancer. He smiled to himself at the thought of someone who would dance to the day, and so, he walked faster to catch up.

As he got closer, he noticed that the figure was that of a young man, and that what he was doing was not dancing at all. The young man was reaching down to the shore, picking up small objects, and throwing them into the ocean.

He came closer still and called out "Good morning! May I ask what it is that you are doing?"

The young man paused, looked up, and replied "Throwing starfish into the ocean."

"I must ask, then, why are you throwing starfish into the ocean?" asked the somewhat startled older man.

To this, the young man replied, "The sun is up and the tide is going out. If I don't throw them in, they'll die."

Upon hearing this, the elderly man commented, "But, young man, don't you realize that there are miles and miles of beach and there are starfish all along every mile? You can't possibly make a difference!"

At this, the young man bent down, picked up yet another starfish, and threw it into the ocean. As it met the water, he said, "It made a difference for that one."

Finding Your Savvy

He who knows others is learned.
He who knows himself is wise.

—Lao Tse

Build your savvy as you learn to

- identify the basics of managing
- assess your current managerial skills
- discover the five savvy managerial competencies
- process information using the L-E-B Model to produce more cohesive actions

Look up the word *savvy* in most any dictionary and you'll find adjectives like sharp, astute, clever, or shrewd. It defines someone with "know-how" who grasps the meaning of things and is acutely perceptive. It is a word that has been used extensively in political circles, and we now offer it to describe someone who is a highly successful manager.

Savvy means more than just following a set of behaviors or action steps. It is a way of being; the manner in which you "show up." A savvy manager delivers solid performance, consistently hits his or her targets, surpasses colleagues on key measurements and results, and attracts top talent. Savvy managers know how to integrate and balance the two competing dimensions of the workplace: the numbers and the people who do the work. As a savvy manager, you have that difficult-to-put-your-finger-on way about you. You seem to be a natural—someone others admire and want to emulate. Being savvy means that you inspire people to excellence, lead ethically, and execute deliberately. Managing this way is a tough act!

■ ■ ■

Real Time: Ryan's Story

Well, this has been an interesting new managers' orientation. Spending a few days with the two other division managers has certainly opened my eyes to a few things.

James manages the consumer products division. He runs a tight ship, something that certainly appeals to my own sense of order and efficiency. I noticed that he's a real stickler for time, watching when his people clock in and how quickly they get to their work stations. Always walking around with that clipboard in his hands seems to have an unsettling effect on his people. I wonder if he even realizes this. During his weekly staff meeting, I noticed that no one questioned him, even on critical issues. I was expecting some comments, but his team only gave nods and OKs to the proposed changes. James confessed to me that he wanted to fire some people, but three of his best employees had given notice over the last few months. He's surprised and frustrated that no one in the company has approached him about those jobs.

Rob, who manages the commercial division, presented me with an entirely different picture. On our first morning together, he walked me around, introducing me to key team leaders. Along the way, he had a smile for everyone and a warm embrace or handshake for those who shared recent team successes. We even stopped to look at the latest pictures of kids and grandkids.

My first impression of Rob was that he seemed too easygoing, too close with his people to be really effective to get results. That opinion totally changed when I saw how he handled his staff meetings. What energy! The level of participation, the give and take, the challenging of ideas and downright arguing were totally intense. It was clear that Rob and his team worked well together, finding solutions and solving problems. He seemed to know just what approach to take with each person, how far to push, when to challenge. I can see why his production numbers are the highest in the company. There is focus, energy, and connection among his people. I've never really noticed that anywhere before and certainly didn't sense it with James's group.

Before this orientation, I never realized how critical my role would be to the success of the division. I see the impact that different styles have on the whole work environment. I need to decide what kind of manager I want to be. What do I need to know? How can I grow into the type of manager where employees flourish?

■ ■ ■

Finding your savvy enables you to become a masterful manager. You enhance your ability to lead, coach, and think both critically and creatively. You refine your complex problem-solving skills. You are able to compete effectively on a global scale, building strategic relationships that engender trust with employees and customers. You master the art of relationship building. You know how to inspire others, enable excellence, and create an environment where your employees are motivated.

Does this sound like the manager that you want to become? We invite you to join us in the pages that follow as we coach you to sharpen your personal game; to take it to the highest, most honorable level of play. The discussions that follow will challenge your thinking at a core level, revealing the underlying reasons that compel you to act the way you do. We will help you shift actions and guide you through the experimenting process of trying new behaviors. You will find your own blind spots and develop new actions that produce better results and more personal satisfaction. Your ability to honestly assess yourself as a manager is an important first step. Here are key questions to help you clarify where you are now and open your thoughts to new learning:

- Are you at the top of your game as a manager?
- Which managerial skills do you use well?
- Which skills need to be further developed?
- Where do you want to go with your career?

The Basics of Managing

Like many people, you may have joined the ranks of management through a promotion. Having acquired proficiency and expertise on the job, you assumed supervisory status, becoming a manager over others. Your promotion affirms a perception of success, your journey up the corporate ladder. It also brings with it a new accountability about how your work is judged and evaluated. Your performance as a manager is no longer determined solely by what you do taskwise but also by your ability to elicit competent work from the people you supervise. We need you to really get this point! Managing people necessitates intricate interpersonal relationships, making it one of the most challenging and rewarding roles in any organization. It is seldom easy, and it is never static. Managing effectively is not for the faint of heart!

> *Management is about human beings.... Its task is to make people capable of joint performance, to make their strengths effective and their weaknesses irrelevant.*
>
> —Peter Drucker

Making the shift from a skilled performer to a manager is a big leap. It requires an internal shift to think and act more collaboratively, inclusively, and globally. Many managers struggle with this shift in thinking for their entire careers. They have difficulty choosing new actions. A manager's inability to work effectively with the human dimension of the company is often blamed for stalling or derailing his or her career. Successful managers possess higher-order people skills, often erroneously referred to as "soft skills." If you have ever managed people, you know that there is nothing "soft" about human relationships, employee performance, and individual and group achievement. Most managers will readily admit that it is the people side that produces sleepless nights and gray hair.

Here is the conundrum. Many managers concentrate their actions in the domains of structure and processes. This includes the key functions of planning, organizing, and controlling that are aligned with rational and linear thinking. Altering how you practice business and serve your customers by adjusting structures and systems can produce higher-productivity payoffs. It is relatively easy to put diagrams on paper, make a flowchart, or announce a system change. However, managing is more that manipulating structure and process through organizational charts, graphs, and business realignments. Addressing structure and process without real thought to employee capabilities and relationships is akin to rearranging the deck chairs on the *Titanic*. You know the ship is in major crisis, yet you don't move beyond the chairs!

The basic management skills you learned in your college management classes—conceptual, analytical, synthesizing, technical, communication, and people skills—are still critically important. We do not discount their value and worth. They are presented for your review in Learning Annex 1 at www.astd.org/SavvyManager. We strongly encourage you to reexamine them, assessing your capabilities to effectively use each one. However, we believe that to become a *savvy* manager, you must be able to grow beyond these basic skills.

The Five Savvy Managerial Skills

Mastery of the five savvy skills described here distinguishes adequate managers from those who become truly great. Savvy managers are *being* managers; they don't just *do* managerial work. The distinction between *being* a manager and just *doing* the functions of a manager are

> *Our experience is not what happens to us but what we make of what happens to us.*
> —Aldous Huxley

developed over time and with practice. As you look at the list, notice that all of the savvy skills focus on both interpersonal and intrapersonal human interactions not processes. These are the competencies that build your confidence, which then fosters your growth to that next level of ability. Our coaching will bring each of these savvy skills into focus and show you when and how to use each one to perfect your development into a great manager. Study the explanation of each skill listed below. As you think about the actions you take, hear our coaching voices asking you this question: *What one change in your own actions might produce a better result?* The five savvy managerial skills are

- self-managing
- reflecting
- acting consciously
- collaborating
- evolving.

Let's look briefly at each of these skills, which you will be encountering again and again throughout the book. Grasping their meaning now will help as you apply them in your own daily practice.

Self-Managing

Your first challenge is to learn how to *manage yourself.* You must know who you are at a gut level. You can't manage yourself if you don't intimately know yourself. Two elements integral to self-managing are self-awareness and self-discipline. Self-awareness, your critical, accurate "I" appraisal, informs who you really are at an internal, private level. Look within. Uncover the issues. Examine the defensive tendencies and bad habits that naturally plague all of us. Often, your outward struggles have deep inner roots that you must have the courage to address to move on. To become a savvy manager, you must recognize your core values and principles. You must be able to uncover the motivations behind your actions. You must fully understand *why* you are doing "x." Becoming aware of your own humanness enables you to strengthen those qualities that serve you best. It is a powerful coaching question that we now ask: *If you cannot manage yourself, how can you ever hope to manage anyone else?*

Self-awareness opens the door to self-managing. You develop personal discipline and control. Self-managing requires you to commit to take actions to diminish behaviors that no longer serve you. Once you can question yourself about your motives and intentions, you develop the discipline to forthrightly deal with the "stuff" that shows up in the actions you take. You also find the courage to take new actions and stick with them, thus enabling new results.

Because the art of managing focuses on human dynamics, it is critically important that you understand who you are and why you do the things you do. Your ability to manage yourself connects to and becomes integrated with the self-management abilities of the people with whom you interact. When the self-management abilities of a group of people all working together are high, amazing results are possible.

> *The most important choice you make is what you choose to make important.*
> —Michael Neill

Conversely, when these abilities are low, people struggle with simple, basic issues at work and in their personal lives. In chapter 3, we further discuss self-awareness and self-management as part of developing your emotional intelligence, a definitive measure of success.

Reflecting

Reflection is the simple practice of quietly contemplating, thinking, and/or observing what has happened without judgment. This next higher-order skill, discussed more fully in the next chapter, asks you to notice what is happening around you and inside of you. Reflection is a quiet practice. Few events can be understood fully as they unfold. It is in that space of reflective thought that previously missed connections between events reveal themselves. Reflection allows for the various layers of complexity to emerge. You gain clarity and a more complete picture. The unknown becomes known.

In truth, most of us think that if we are still and just thinking, not doing "something," then we are wasting time. The fast pace of life and business affairs seldom allows quiet, reflective time. Therefore, you must consciously make both the time and extend the effort to reflect. Take a moment now to ascertain how well you undertake any reflective practice.

Establish a reflection practice at specific points during your day. Before you leave work at the end of the day, stop and reflect for a few minutes. Consider what went well and what did not follow the path you had planned. Use your insights to set your intentions for what you want to change and/or accomplish the next day. Pay attention to things going on around you and within you to deepen your understanding of the connections among events, emotions, thoughts, and actions.

Acting Consciously

For many people, the act of making a choice is one of the most difficult of all skills. It is so difficult that many never do it! Rather, they allow external circumstances to take control without any conscious intervention. *Acting consciously*, the third savvy skill, focuses on your ability to wisely choose your actions. It is all about being fully aware of your choices and how you actually choose. Acting consciously demands higher-level conceptual thinking, which flows from your ability to generate possible alternatives.

Acting consciously means that you deliberately and intentionally select from viable options. If your choice shows itself to be flawed or misdirected as events unfold, you then consciously work through the thought process again from that new vantage point. You recognize that choosing is a fluid process of unparalleled learning focused on what works and what does not work in real time.

Your goal here is to develop your competency to make conscious choices more aligned with the outcomes you really want. Clearly understand at this point that you always have a choice about what to think, what to say, and how to act. This realization is the most profound lesson you can learn. Savvy managers appreciate the risk-reward equation associated with having control in decisions. They find choosing highly empowering.

Collaborating

Collaborating is the work platform of the 21st century. It is the epitome of the "we" workplace, where extending respect and excellent service to fellow workers is the foundation of all interactions. Collaboration takes advantage of the most effective actions possible because it focuses on and utilizes the unique gifts and strengths of the many. Everyone's skills complement and reinforce one another's. Collaboration creates an energy that inspires and motivates. Through collaboration, people gain a stronger appreciation for how their efforts align, add value, and produce results for the company.

> *If you want to build a ship, don't herd people together to collect wood and don't be so rigid to assign tasks and work, but rather teach them to long for the immensity of the sea.*
>
> —Antoine de Saint-Exupéry

Imagine yourself as an orchestra conductor—only, you are orchestrating the efforts of your own team. You carefully select worthwhile projects that will resonate with employees. Clearly defined, measurable goals serve as targets and benchmarks for project teams. You establish the framework (decision-making process, feedback loop, communications network) within which the work will be done before any work gets started. And, most important, you choose talent carefully, looking for people with both essential technical skills and the relationship skills critical to the success of the collaborative effort.

One more point about collaboration is pertinent. Savvy managers know that collaboration requires employees to be part of something larger than themselves—a project with meaning and importance. To that end, they artfully help employees relinquish ego behaviors, replacing them with mutually beneficial ones. They act consciously to ensure that every person knows how much his or her contribution adds to the project's success. As companies move to more virtual projects executed globally, utilizing a host of virtual communication technologies, collaboration challenges will intensify. Building your collaborating skill allows you to handle disparate work spread across various cultures and time zones and to transcend various boundaries. It becomes your strategy for bringing out the best in each person.

Evolving

The final savvy skill is to *evolve*. Evolving necessitates continually applying the lessons you learn to every significant experience in your life. It means that you assume full accountability for your own growth and development. You constantly seek new learning opportunities that enable your effectiveness with both systems (the science) and people (the art) to refine your managerial craft. Your nemesis, complacency, must be intercepted and replaced with a commitment to your own growth.

The process of evolving begins with an attitude that supports self-development and professional growth. You have to have a hunger for more! It also is tied to the vision you hold of yourself and what is truly possible for you. If you think you are already at the top of your game, then there really is no place for you to grow. But if you believe that you have yet to produce your best work, regardless of where you are, you open the door to possibilities. You have to see and believe that you can be more, do more, and have what you envision for your career and, therefore, your life. You also have to give yourself permission to take calculated risks to expand your skills and competencies.

Your starting point for evolving is to uncover and reflect on any limitations that you believe about yourself or that others have placed upon you that you hold true. Reexamine what you tell yourself you can and cannot do. Do you see yourself in a positive, healthy way and view life as meaningful and worthwhile? Do you seek opportunities to build strong relationships or shy away from them? Tap into your creativity. Evolving is part of the whole process of Abraham Maslow's self-actualizing (Maslow 1998). You come to realize that life is about finding more fulfillment from being your best self. The essence of our coaching through the chapters that follow will center around helping you grow and evolve into a savvy manager and an exceptional human being.

Table 1-1 pulls all the savvy skills we are introducing together and adds a savvy translation to help you think about new actions to take. Clearly, you cannot do it all at once, so begin slowly. Our coaching suggestion is to start with self-managing, because the other savvy skills all have their roots tied to how well you can manage yourself.

X Marks the Spot!

How do *you* process and internalize information? For most of us, this happens through the interplay of three learning domains—language, emotions, and body—presented visually as the L-E-B Model (figure 1-1). The L-E-B Model offers you a way to understand how you take action. From this realization, you can incorporate the five savvy managerial skills more effectively as you manage yourself and your team.

Here is how it works. You collect data mentally through language, emotionally from feelings and moods, and as physical and biological responses. In the process, you give meaning to all the things you see, hear, think, feel, and experience. You create interpretations, which lead you to make decisions about what actions to take or avoid. And all this happens in a nanosecond!

Think about a recent interaction with your boss, employees, or co-workers. The interaction probably took place within the mental domain of language. This domain, the most common entry for information, includes talking, listening, reading, and writing. Processing information, understanding ideas and concepts, reflecting and assimilating occur as we *think* through and assign meaning to words and sounds and the mental images that emerge.

Table 1-1. Savvy Management Skills

Skill	Conceptual Focus	Savvy Translation
Self-Managing	Clearly knowing who you are allows you to stay focused and act with confidence. Discipline and control come directly from self-awareness.	Savvy managers really know themselves and use this knowing to their advantage. They have a personal discipline and focus that give confidence and power to the actions they take. Others find comfort in the strength they witness and respond well.
Reflecting	Reflection lets you notice what is happening or has happened, without moving to judgment.	Savvy managers understand the power of silent observation. Stepping back from the action, even as it is surrounding them, gives them clarity that enables more powerful actions.
Acting Consciously	Choices are made every moment of the day. Even when you choose to do nothing, you are actually making a choice. Making choices more consciously, with an outcome in mind, strengthens your decisions.	Savvy managers come from a place of intentional action. Choices are made after thought and consideration of options. They know that real success lives in the act of choosing.
Collaborating	Working with the full involvement of people means inviting them to contribute their best to the project in ways that inspire.	Savvy managers seek out talent unencumbered by boundaries, like job descriptions or titles. They know their success is embedded in their ability to harness and empower the contributions of many.
Evolving	Continuing to grow and hone your managerial talents moves you to higher levels of performance and greater satisfaction.	Savvy managers know they are only as successful as their ability to learn and grow. Stagnation and complacency mean death. To be alive is to evolve.

> *Learning is about being different and moving in new ways in your world.*
>
> —Julio Olalla

You also processed the interaction above within your emotional domain. This includes feelings, emotions, attitudes, and your underlying motivation. Just as your mental domain was alerted to the words and meanings, your emotional domain was triggered by the feelings the words evoked. Depending on the specific interaction, your feelings ran the gamut from nonplussed to highly volatile. Everyone has emotional triggers—those words or actions of others or those events that unfold on a daily basis. Your emotional domain is part of your prevailing mood and all-around perspective on life.

Figure 1-1. The L-E-B Model

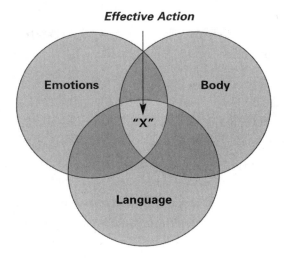

Effective Action

Emotions

Body

"X"

Language

Source: Used by permission of Newfield Network, Inc.

Although Don Vito Corleone said "It's not personal, it's just business," the fact is that it is almost impossible to separate words and actions from the emotions they evoke. Consider the feedback you receive from your interactions with others. Regardless of whether your performance gets criticized or praised, your interpretation of this feedback, and the resulting emotion, has an impact on how you assimilate the information. Criticism may cause resentment and impede your actions, or it might stimulate you to rise to the challenge and improve your performance. Genuine praise most often fosters growth.

The third point of entry for information includes physical and biological responses. Again, examining the same event from above, did you notice any physical reaction? Just as criticism and praise produce emotional responses, they can also elicit physical reactions. Criticism might cause your jaw to become rigid, heat (blush or perspiration) to rise in your body, or a knot to form in your stomach. Praise might bring a smile, cause you to blush, and release pressure points in your shoulders or neck. Genuine praise can create a glow in your physical being. The information you receive from the physical domain plays an equally important role in how you interpret and respond to interactions with others.

In figure 1-1, the "X" at the center of all three L-E-B circles marks that highest point of your emerging capability to act cohesively, with savvy. Effective action always results from the alignment of what you think, what you say, how you feel, and what you do. Just think about the last time you verbally said "yes" to something but were thinking "no." You were not aligned! Your ability to pull the circles closer together, thereby making the center "X" space larger, is the objective. It is directly connected to your ability to more effectively reflect upon and integrate your interpretations of events.

Your coaching here is aimed at growing your awareness of how you move from interpretation to action. The goal is to allow the process to become more holistic and cohesive. Your challenge is to work through your interpretations of events and then use your budding savvy skills to take more effective action. For example, in any given situation, you might stop before you react, reflect on both what has occurred and what you really want to happen next, and take more conscious action. Your newly created alignment produces a wealth of interpretations and possibilities. Your authentic self now interacts more powerfully with the world.

 Savvy Translation: Savvy managers know that the greatest effectiveness occurs when the three domains of language, emotions, and body are aligned. They focus their efforts to hone everyone's conscious ability to pull these domains of learning together for themselves, thereby enabling peak performance from all players.

The Bottom Line: Finding Your Savvy

Savvy managers understand that work has moved beyond the utilitarian, scientific principles of management. And although they recognize and apply the marvelous benefits of process and technology, they know that human interaction and performance produce the greater return-on-investment. The five savvy managerial skills form the foundation for what you need to manage in our changing times. These skills offer you the opportunity to propel your organization toward higher levels of performance and to be more successful personally.

So it begins for you! When first viewed, these five savvy skills may appear simple and practical. But as you begin to implement them, you will realize the effort required to master them. In the beginning, assimilating these skills will take more time and dedication, as you weigh and consider your decisions and actions. Practice will become your partner for success.

Your accountability as a manager asks you to develop skills to work with each person, as both a unique individual and one among many. It is an exercise of blending separate and together. As you get wiser about the intricate, interpersonal relationships with employees and the culture of the group, you inspire people to achieve great things. Savvy managers become obsessive, in a positive way, to bring out the best performance from themselves and others.

If you accept the challenges of becoming a savvy manager, you must utilize all your resources in ways that inspire the best from the people side of the organization and to connect it with highly optimized, productive processes on the systems side. Your final coaching question for this chapter asks you to dig deep within yourself. *Do you have the courage and perseverance to synthesize these new skills and discover a different way of thinking and being as a manager?*

Use It or Lose It
Write down the one key idea that you "got" as a takeaway from your reading. Then write down what you plan to do starting tomorrow to integrate this idea, practice it, and make it a habit.

1. What I got. _____

   _____

2. How I will use it tomorrow. _____

   _____

3. Which savvy skill(s) I am developing. _____

   _____

Reflection Interval
As you read the short story below, think about the skills you are building with your thoughts and your actions. Are these the skills you want to build? Are these the skills you need to get to where you want to go with your career—with your life?

The Cathedral
By Charles M. Schwab, founder of Bethlehem Steel

Three men were laying brick.

The first was asked, "What are you doing?"

He answered, "Laying some brick."

The second man was asked, "What are you working for?"

He answered, "Five dollars a day."

The third man was asked, "What are you doing?"

He answered, "I am helping to build a great cathedral."

Which man are you?

Coaching for Action: Driving Optimal Performance

New Skills for Managers

1. Wander around your organization and identify which managers are clearly integrating the specific new *savvy* skills we are discussing in this chapter. Can you identify areas where these savvy skills are missing or most needed?

2. Take a specific issue confronting you at work. Which of your current skills are helping you deal with this issue? Which savvy skills do you need to develop to enable you to be more effective with respect to this issue?

Acting Cohesively

1. Think of a specific situation confronting you at work. Draw the three circles of the L-E-B Model. Under the diagram, make three columns and label them language, emotions, and body.

2. Write down the language you are using when you describe the situation, the emotions you are experiencing, and how you are holding your body in relation to this situation.

3. Keeping in mind that the meaning you place on events, your interpretation, determines the action that you think you can take, write down what actions you believe to be possible.

4. Are you getting the result you want? If not, how would your interpretations have to change to realize the desired results? Your interpretive meaning leads to your evaluation of the situation, which leads to your decisions about possible actions, which leads to your actual actions, which lead to your results.

Assessing Your Savvy

Ready for that introspective look? Conduct your own personal skills assessment.

1. Use worksheet 1-1 to assess your current capabilities for each new savvy skill introduced in this chapter. Use the 1-to-7 scale, with 1 being poor skill development and 7 representing outstanding skill development. Circle the number that you think represents your level of capability with the skill.

2. For the "Moving to Mastery" column, think about the number you circled and what it would take for you to move just one number higher. For example, if you rated yourself a 5 in self-management, what would you have to commit to doing differently to move your self-assessment to a 6? Write your new behaviors in the "Moving to Mastery" column.

3. Choose one skill to focus on for the next week. As you move through each day of the week, be conscious about the actions you are taking. Think before you act. Make choices that align with moving your chosen skill assessment to the next-higher number. Notice the results you get.

4. Repeat this same process for each of the new savvy skills. For the best results, confine yourself to one new skill each week. The point is to shift your behaviors to allow new practices to take root. When you have worked through each skill one time, go back and begin the process again.

Worksheet 1-1. Assessing Your Savvy

Savvy Skill	Rating	Moving to Mastery: New Behaviors
Self-Managing	1 2 3 4 5 6 7	
Reflecting	1 2 3 4 5 6 7	
Acting Consciously	1 2 3 4 5 6 7	
Collaborating	1 2 3 4 5 6 7	
Evolving	1 2 3 4 5 6 7	

Savvy Skill Development Record

Week of	
Skill focus	
Actions	
Observations	

Discovering Your Prism of Perception

The true journey of discovery does not consist in searching for new territories but in having new eyes.

—Marcel Proust

Build your savvy as you learn to

- analyze how perceptual filters shape your thoughts and actions
- discover how the power of perception impacts performance
- incorporate the position of observer to change habits and achieve results
- apply tools to develop your perceptual capabilities

Now that we have introduced you to the five savvy skills that enable you to more effectively manage both processes and people, we must delve more deeply into the arena of thought. Most specifically, we focus on your ability to think differently. To access more expansive thinking, you must build fresh awareness of how you assign meaning to events and how these meanings ultimately affect your performance and career success. Remember, your thoughts direct your actions. In this chapter, we expose your "meaning-making" mechanisms. Our goal is to assist you in exploring new ways to manage your perceptions. As you learn how to consciously see what you think, your ability to take more effective actions expands. Two critical elements come to the forefront for your learning: perception and observation.

■ ■ ■

Real Time: Robin's Story

I'm really confused. I thought things were going so well for us. I worked hard getting ready for yesterday morning's staff meeting. I wrote my notes carefully and then rewrote them to make sure I was clear about the ideas I wanted to stress to the team. Everyone seemed attentive during my presentation. Lots of heads were nodding, people were smiling, and everyone seemed to be following my vision of where we were heading this year. Although I did most of the talking, the few comments I got from people afterward were very positive and aligned around my key points. Wow! What a difference a day makes. Now, 24 hours later and I have a whole new set of challenges confronting me. Wasn't anyone listening yesterday?

Carl, my business manager, informed me that two account managers pulled him aside after the meeting to complain that I was just "beating up" on them and their department. They just don't get how I could make comments about our customer relationships and not see that I was not making a dig against them.

Mary sent me an email this morning detailing her plans to run with the ideas I shared at the meeting. I love her enthusiasm, but what she's proposing seems out of alignment with the direction I thought I had so carefully crafted. I know she was listening, but I'm beginning to wonder what happened when my words got translated into "Mary language." And John left me a voicemail saying he wants to set up a face-to-face to clear up some of his concerns around my plans. I have no problem meeting with him, but he seems to be taking exception to something that wasn't even addressed.

The tension in the office is really high. No one is making eye contact with me. Even the employees who normally see "the cup as half full" are moaning and complaining. The naysayers have certainly dug in their heels, totally prepared for doom and gloom. I don't understand how so many people could be in the same room, hear the same thing, and leave with totally different interpretations.

My talk was a vision piece, more directional than detailed. Sharing my vision for our department was supposed to stimulate and inspire everyone. Where did I go wrong in my presentation? How could I have been clearer? More important, what can I do to fix this?

■ ■ ■

Like the prism that bursts a light spectrum into myriad colors, the observer that you are filters your world into infinite possibilities. Utilizing the savvy skills of self-management, reflection, and acting consciously, you refine your ability to perceive the full scope of the situation before you ever take action. When you step into the role of observer, and couple it with more evolved perceptual skills, you can begin to really see beyond the obvious. Once you can more clearly identify the roots of your actions and recognize why you do what you do, you can begin to make more informed connections. You realize the relationships between your thoughts and the conclusions that lead to your choices, which then direct your actions. It is from a more developed and complete understanding of an event that you make distinctions, ask insightful questions of yourself and others, and add clarity to your thinking.

> *From quiet reflection will come even more effective action.*
> —Peter Drucker

Your coaching here concentrates on several unique process tools developed by key management thinkers of our time. Incorporating these tools into your everyday actions will enable you to better manage your perceptions to generate the outcomes you really want. The first tool examines the role of the observer. Using this model, you expose the filters and blinders through which you see your own world. Then the ladder of inference allows you to map the transparent process you follow as you assign meaning to events and situations. Finally, we walk you through the five managerial mindsets that will permit you to step into different thinking modes in any situation, increasing your intellectual versatility and ability to act consciously.

The Power of Perception

To help visualize the rather ethereal concept of perception, think about an apparently still pond of water. Despite the appearance of stillness, there is activity occurring below the surface. Nothing is really completely still. Now, picture a stone being thrown into that pond. The ripples flow outward from the stone's point of entry, disturbing the surface of the water, altering the patterns of movement both above and below. You can see the energy released on top of the water but can only surmise what is happening below. As you watch the ripples move outward from the point of entry, you see small symmetrical, calming ripples. Someone else watching this same scene might describe the ripples as varied, erratic, and dizzying. The power of perception produces different descriptions from watching the same scenario of a stone tossed into the pond. In this visualization, recognize that you are the pond, events are the stones, and your perceptions are the ripples.

> *Every man takes the limits of his own field of vision for the limits of the world.*
>
> —Arthur Schopenhauer

Your perceptions are the unique interpretation of your reality at any given moment. They function as your window to the world, giving meaning to events and shaping your thoughts and emotions. Everything that happens to you gets processed through transparent filters that you selectively apply. Your perceptual filters establish the context within which you give meaning to events. These filters include past experiences, feelings, personal biases, and selective exposure. For example, a negative annual review from your past may have you dreading an upcoming evaluation, even though you know your current performance has been right on target. You may be avoiding co-workers with lots of facial body piercing or tattoos because of the stereotyping or prejudicial filters you hold. Your filters also are based on expectations, wants, needs, and goals. Because you are hoping for a raise, you might take a comment from your boss that "the third-quarter numbers look good" as a sign of a pending bonus.

All of us tend to believe that our perceptions are reality. They give us a picture of the world not as it is but as how we think it is. Most of us will work tirelessly to prove that our perceptions are accurate to validate our feelings or justify our actions. Because perceptions shape how you discern and interpret events, they play a huge role in your life and in your career. Think about yourself and your own tendencies. Be brutally honest. How do you process your world? Are your perceptions processed through negative filters of what could go wrong or might be a major obstacle? Maybe your filters are always positive and optimistic, seeing potential or possibility. You could be a facts-and-figures person who wants and needs hard, proven data to process information. Or perhaps you are inclined to use your senses and feelings, emotionally filtering events from the "gut." Each of us has a tendency to use certain filters as our standard operating procedure in life.

It is critical that you not only learn to recognize which filters you are using in any given situation but also that you consciously self-manage how you use information filtered in any certain way. Monitor your perceptual filters. Fully translate how they shape your thought patterns and influence your feelings in approaching events and making decisions. It is equally important that you recognize that you have the power to control and alter your perceptions. In doing so, you open yourself to thinking differently, which allows a host of new possibilities to emerge.

As a manager, you have the additional challenge to understand how your employees use their different perceptual filters when approaching situations. Through reflection, you first realize how your employees are filtering events. Using your savvy skill of collaboration,

> *The pessimist sees difficulty in every opportunity. The optimist sees the opportunity in every difficulty.*
> —Winston Churchill

you help your employees take more effective actions. To accomplish this, you validate their beliefs and open dialogue and discussion. You check for all the different shades of meaning that might be emerging from their perceptions. You use this insight to enhance comprehension, foster synergy, and ultimately align performance and actions among the members of your team.

Consider Joan, for example. Her company has gone through a major restructuring in recent months. Some employees have been downsized, while others are being offered new challenges and responsibilities. Like many remaining employees, Joan feels lost and uncertain about her future with the company. This uncertainty has begun to show up in her performance as poor attention to details and a somewhat cavalier attitude to customers. Her manager, Sam, notices a change in her demeanor. Rather than ignoring it, he approaches Joan for an open and honest conversation. He learns that she is worried that she will be the next person to be "let go." Her fears and the pressure of losing her job are causing sleepless nights and high stress.

Sam asks Joan to question her belief in light of the company's most recent memo sharing its new goals in its current market position. He shares with her a service complaint from a customer. He helps her recognize the impact of her work to the company and on her professional reputation. He has taken the time to understand her perceptions, validate them, and help her reframe. And Joan has been able to address what is within her control and to assess her own performance and recognize its impact on her company's profitability.

The most significant point to take away from this discussion of perception is the powerful link it has to performance. As a manager, you must recognize that all performance is guided by perception. You need to realize that you cannot change performance in another person until that person changes or aligns his or her perceptions about his or her performance. You must do your managerial work behind the scenes. You must monitor perceptions and their alignment with performance and take action when something appears out of line. Results that better serve everyone are possible when perceptions are aligned.

Savvy Translation: Savvy managers recognize the power of perceptions on performance. They consciously operate where others fear to
tread, asking questions that challenge thoughts and perceptions to
open up new possibilities for action.

The Role of the Observer

Observing is reflection in real time. Because perception is fundamental to performance, you must pay closer attention to how you see and, subsequently, interpret
events. This is about learning to become mindful, aware, and present. Mindfulness,
a unique state of being present in the moment, demands that you pay attention
without the impact of biases or judgments. You simply focus and notice the observable relationship of actions and results.

It works this way: You perform an action and get a result. If your action creates the
result you want, you continue the action. If the action does not create the result you
want, or you want different results, you choose a new action. The action loop thus
is action, result, action, result—as shown in figure 2-1. Over time, a transparent
action-result loop gets embedded and becomes routine. You repeat what is comfortable and familiar, which then gets labeled as habit. Even when you might desire a
different result, your comfort zone with the habit controls your actions. The action
result cycle becomes a habitual process.

Most people fail to realize when they have become trapped in a loop. Picture a
classic Wile E. Coyote and Road Runner chase sequence from Saturday morning

Figure 2-1. Traditional Action-Result Loop

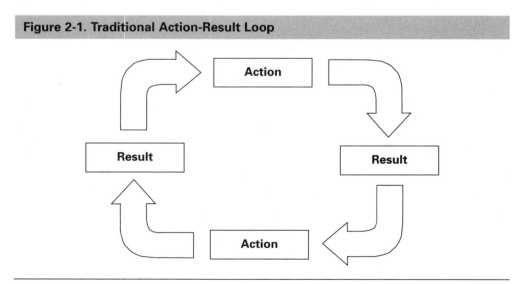

Source: Adapted from Newfield Network Inc.

cartoons. It doesn't take long before Road Runner jumps on a nearby rock while Wile E. Coyote chases endlessly in circles, not realizing that Road Runner is no longer in the chase. Wile E. Coyote has become stuck in his habitual action-result loop. In this loop, he can't even "see" the need to change his behavior. Hence, the same chase sequence ensues, albeit at different locales.

To change a habit and get new results requires a new model. This operational model, depicted in figure 2-2, adds a moderating position. The added first position becomes one of observation. Observation is defined as focused attention or interpretative watching. It is almost like having an out-of-body experience, where you pause and step back from the action. You give yourself time to see what is happening. In the observer role, you notice events, perform assessments, validate feelings, and weigh alternatives.

Adding the observer position allows you to become more aware of your perceptual filters. You create a neutral point, a space to disengage from action, to evaluate what is happening before continuing to any possible next action. This

> *Observe all men—thyself most.*
> —Ben Franklin

space can be as fast as a breath or as long as a walk in the park. A coaching point here is to recognize that while you are the observer, at the same time you are a participating force in what is being observed. Remember that your frame of reference, experience base, biases, and prejudices all come into play as you observe events. Your question then becomes *Who is the observer doing the observing?*

Figure 2-2. Observer Model

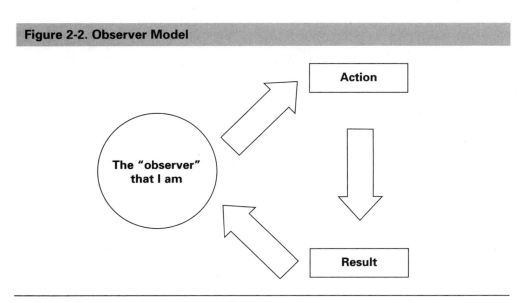

Source: Adapted from Newfield Network Inc.

Through the practice of observation, you learn how to see beyond the obvious, to make distinctions, ask questions, and consider new actions. Utilizing this process, you uncover facts and separate them from opinions and assessments, adding clarity and depth to your thought process, as shown in figure 2-3. You play "what if" scenarios that simulate changes to your perspective and point of view. When you honestly begin to explore the observer that you are, you can truly illuminate and then challenge and test those assumptions.

Savvy Translation: Savvy managers embrace the role of observer. They make every effort to fully see what is happening and to routinely question and test their assumptions.

Enhancing Perceptual Skills

Two effective tools will build your perceptual capabilities and increase your capacity to think in new directions. The first tool is called the ladder of inference. As developed by several well-known management theorists (Senge et al. 1994), the ladder of inference exposes the progression of an event through the unique meaning-making process of individual interpretation. The second tool describes five lenses or mindsets through which to view the ever-changing business landscape (Mintzberg and Gosling 2003).

The Ladder of Inference

Understanding how you attach meaning to events is an important step in managing perceptions and taking more effective actions. Look at the ladder of inference

Figure 2-3. "What's Happening" Interpretations

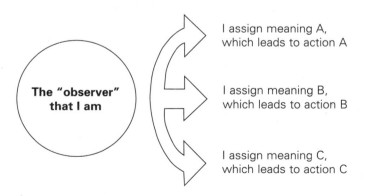

shown in figure 2-4 to better appreciate the steps you follow to create your story about events as they unfold. This is a process that takes place in a nanosecond. It reveals your path and your mental gymnastics as you create an event-to-meaning connection.

Using figure 2-4, follow along as we describe the internal process that occurs as you advance up the six rungs of the ladder of inference. The lowest rung contains the actual observable data that you see and hear. At the second rung, selective exposure and selective listening occur. Your personal filters and agenda begin to make adjustments to what you have seen and heard. Your inner systems are trying to make the new data fit. Information outside your scope of reference is invisible to you and does not move up the ladder. On rung three, your filtered data is further refined and gets assigned meaning based on your personal, cultural, and organizational belief systems. An important point to recognize about this third rung is that the belief systems you use for evaluative purposes come from past experiences. Again, the concept of fit comes into play.

Rung four of the ladder of inference is the level of assumption. You presume and create your realities based on the meaning and belief systems that were in play in rung three. These assumptions lead you to rung five, where you draw conclusions directly from your assumptions. Rung six is about taking action. The actions you now choose come directly from conclusions you formulated from assumptions made from the meanings you assigned to the data you allowed into your purview. That is your journey up this ladder.

Figure 2-4. Ladder of Inference

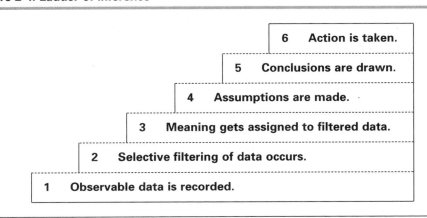

Source: Adapted from Senge et al (1994, 243).

This experience of climbing the ladder of inference is transparent and happens instantaneously. A real work situation, described in the following paragraphs, can help you better understand the events that occur in moving up the ladder of inference. Notice in the examples how two people take two completely different paths in assigning meaning, drawing conclusions, and taking action with the exact same information.

At a regular department meeting, the manager, Vanessa, asks her staff to "pay closer attention to expenses" during the upcoming quarter. Through Ben's filters, this translates into salary cuts. After all, that's what happened when his previous employer talked about paying closer attention to expenses. Although Vanessa said nothing about salaries, Ben assigns this meaning here and concludes that he is going to get a crummy raise. His story becomes one of greedy management "sticking it" to employees one more time! Thinking that rewards and compensation are limited, he allows his performance to deteriorate to "doing just enough to get by."

Ben's co-worker Mark hears the same information from Vanessa. He filters it as the company wanting to simply monitor and control expenses. He embraces the challenge to do his part. He begins to verify departmental spending and negotiate more aggressively with vendors, seeking the best deals possible. Mark's story, in contrast to Ben's story, is one of teamwork and collaborative efforts for the greater good of all.

Ben and Mark—same meeting, same information; but different perceptions, different responses! Check your own ladder of inference. Listen the next time you make a strong statement about something that you believe to be true. Maybe you say, "Management does not care about employees" or "My company treats me with a great deal of respect." The beliefs that underlie these perceptions have a direct impact on your actions. Self-manage and challenge your belief systems in light of current information to grow and find new possibilities. Reflecting will let you discern, isolate, and really "out" your own filters. Consciously choose actions that produce the outcomes you really want. You always have a choice! Be selective and take appropriate actions. Avoid the pull of a downward spiral that serves no one.

 Savvy Translation: Savvy managers develop the ability to expose their perceptual meaning-making filters. They know that this critical skill requires time and attention, which they recognize and embrace as a managerial accountability.

Five Mindsets

Think back to the basketball game Around the World that you might have played as a child. Each shot would be taken from different positions, moving you around the center key. Each position offered you a different sight on the basket. It required just a slight adjustment in how you would shoot to drop the ball into the hoop. It took focus and skill to master each position for that perfect shot.

Enter five mindsets, which let you play Around the World in your organization, only in your head without the basketball. These five thinking methods or five mindsets—reflective, analytical, worldly, collaborative, and action—help you make adjustments to sharpen your perceptions. These mindsets were articulated by management scholars Henry Mintzberg and Jonathan Gosling (2003). Unlike traditional managerial approaches, which view the organization as discrete operational functions (accounting, marketing, operations, and the like), Mintzberg and Gosling call for a shift in perspective. Their mindsets afford a more integrative way of visioning your organization—its issues, events, and opportunities—to take more decisive and deliberate actions. Managing in complex and changing times demands these powerful competencies. Let's take a look at each mindset.

> *Nothing changes without personal transformation.*
> —W. Edwards Deming

The Reflective Mindset

The first mindset, the reflective, centers on self-knowledge and is directly connected to the savvy skills of self-managing and reflecting. Knowing yourself allows you to see how the processing of events, information, and the actions you take or avoid are inextricably tied to your self-concept. When you step back and reflect, it stirs emotions and conjures new images about how events connect to that place inside you. Gaining clarity about yourself and becoming comfortable in your own skin helps you understand how your perceptions lead to the choices you make.

Because it touches on issues that you may have buried deeply and want to ignore, the reflective mindset is often neglected. However, from every action you take and those actions you choose to avoid, the practice of reflecting brings hidden issues to the surface. Often, they are ancient events that can be holding your personal and professional advancement hostage. Once visible, you can take action to deal with these issues. What a gift! Make time to reflect. It is where you learn more about yourself and can make changes that serve you now and for the future.

The Analytical Mindset

The second mindset, the analytical, focuses on the inner workings of the organization. Analysis asks you to break events and situations into smaller components. Doing this takes time, and it requires the concurrent ability to see from different vantage points. This is where different business functions come into play. *How would your marketing person view this situation? How would a financial person analyze this information? What would the human resources department have to say?* Once you develop the ability to think from different viewpoints, you can more easily recognize how to change your actions, be more collaborative, and get better results.

The Worldly Mindset

A third mindset, the worldly, gives meaning to the statement that nothing exists in isolation. It accesses your ability to fully and completely examine the environment, to see the bigger picture in making decisions. The worldly mindset helps you deal with key topics like outsourcing and globalization, both vital considerations in an expanding economy and for the viability of any business. With a worldly mindset, you uncover your blind spots and fully evaluate situations on a more global level.

The Collaborative Mindset

The fourth mindset, the collaborative, explores working relationships. Teamwork, trust, communication, power, and leadership are all elements that converge in this mindset. It goes beyond just establishing norms of behavior and compliance; it is more than just cooperating with employees. The collaborative mindset requires intentions to fully include all parties, a commitment to mutually beneficial outcomes, and the full engagement of and accountability by everyone to achieve those results.

The Action Mindset

The fifth mindset, action, is about acting within the ever-present reality of change. The action mindset occurs as the final sequence in the saying "Ready, aim, fire!" It directs everyone to action. It focuses on execution that is purposeful, timely, and goal directed. Learning how your organization deals with its action challenges encompasses both macro issues (the organization as a whole) and micro issues (the individuals). You need to discover how this action mindset emerges for you in your experiences at work.

Summing Up the Five Mindsets

The five mindsets come full circle as you reflect on your actions. Reflecting after action, you might ask these questions: *Did you get what you wanted from the actions you took? What might still be missing? Did the costs balance the returns? What's next?* All functions of management are involved here as integrated elements of a common whole. No one perspective controls or wields more influence to the detriment of the others. Working through the five mindsets offers you a systematic and effective process to function synergistically in an environment of constant change. The higher the synergy, the more productive the action, the better the results.

As you examine table 2-1, think of a situation you face right now at work. Adopt each mindset, one by one, focusing on your situation or problem from that perspective or lens. Pay particular attention to the savvy translation to help you gain clarity and understanding. Your coaching focus here is to see if you can link the *observer* that you are to Mintzberg and Gosling's mindsets to reveal a more insightful you, who is able to think and perform in new ways.

Table 2-1. Savvying Up Mintzberg and Gosling's Mindset

Mindset	Conceptual Focus	Savvy Skills	Savvy Translation
Reflective	Self-knowledge	Self-Managing, Reflecting	You can only understand the world when you first take time to fully understand yourself in relation to the world. Savvy managers take the time to know who they are completely and how they "fit."
Analytical	Inner workings of the organization	Self-Managing, Reflecting, Acting Consciously	Savvy managers recognize the reality of every situation and are able to connect with that reality in their choice of actions. They know that without the ability to analyze what is happening, choosing actions is a crap shoot.
Worldly	Big-picture thinking	Reflecting, Acting Consciously, Evolving	Coming from a perspective of possibility, savvy managers envision new futures and a broad range of alternative paths of action. They think globally and inclusively.
Collaborative	Working relationships, commitment	Self-Managing, Reflecting, Collaborating	Trust is the operative word for a savvy manager. Savvy managers make commitments that honor all people, regardless of how challenging this is in actual practice. Integrity supports all their efforts.
Action	Taking action	Self-Managing, Acting Consciously, Collaborating	Savvy managers know that the constancy of action undergirds everything. *"What's next?"* is the rallying cry. Each meeting and discussion ends with forward movement.

Source: Adapted from Mintzberg and Gosling (2003).

The Bottom Line: Discovering Your Prism of Perception

As part of advancing your savvy skills, we've challenged you to consider your perceptions as a critical dimension to your outcomes and the way that you manage yourself and your team. As you more fully appreciate the power your perceptions have to influence events, you increase your ability to act consciously. Reflecting on what you think increases your clarity. It allows you to suspend old concepts, staid ideas, and habitual responses that no longer serve you. You open the door to greater intellectual versatility and more innovative thinking.

With these new tools, you can better peel back the layers to challenge current interpretations and reveal different perspectives of the same visible reality. This practice empowers thinking. It either reinforces that you are on the right track or shows you the disconnects. Collaborative action comes from shared understandings and respect for differences. It happens when you clearly express your perceptions of events and allow others to do the same. Your bottom-line accountability as a manager is to create the environment that fosters speaking one's truth. It begins with the recognition that each person holds his or her *perception* of the truth.

Use It or Lose It

Write down the one key idea that you "got" as a takeaway from your reading. Then write down what you plan to do starting tomorrow to integrate this idea, practice it, and make it a habit.

1. What I got. _____

   _____

2. How I will use it tomorrow. _____

   _____

3. Which savvy skill(s) I am developing._____

   _____

Reflection Interval

As you read the story below, think about your own habits of appraising events and situations in your life. Is there a blind man in you who only sees part of the whole? Can you create a new you who is more open to different perspectives and willing to really see all the parts?

The Parable of the Blind Men and the Elephant
The original version is from a Buddhist text

A number of disciples went to the Buddha and said, "Sir, there are living here in Savatthi many wandering hermits and scholars who indulge in constant dispute, some saying that the world is infinite and eternal and others that it is finite and not eternal, some saying that the soul dies with the body and others that it lives on forever, and so forth. What, Sir, would you say concerning them?"

The Buddha answered, "Once upon a time there was a certain raja who called to his servant and said, 'Come, good fellow, go and gather together in one place all the men of Savatthi who were born blind, ...and show them an elephant.' 'Very good, sire,' replied the servant, and he did as he was told. He said to the blind men assembled there, 'Here is an elephant,' and to one man he presented the head of the elephant, to another its ears, to another a tusk, to another the trunk, the foot, back, tail, and tuft of the tail, saying to each one that that was the elephant.

"When the blind men had felt the elephant, the raja went to each of them and said to each, 'Well, blind man, have you seen the elephant? Tell me, what sort of thing is an elephant?'

"Thereupon the men who were presented with the head answered, 'Sire, an elephant is like a pot.' And the men who had observed the ear replied, 'An elephant is like a winnowing basket.' Those who had been presented with a tusk said it was a ploughshare. Those who knew only the trunk said it was a plough; others said the body was a granary; the foot, a pillar; the back, a mortar; the tail, a pestle; the tuft of the tail, a brush.

"Then they began to quarrel, shouting, 'Yes it is!' 'No, it is not!' 'An elephant is not that!' 'Yes, it's like that!' and so on, until they came to blows over the matter.

"Brethren, the raja was delighted with the scene.

"Just so are these preachers and scholars holding various views blind and unseeing.... In their ignorance, they are by nature quarrelsome, wrangling, and disputatious, each maintaining reality is thus and thus."

> Then the Exalted One rendered this meaning by uttering this verse of uplift:
>
> "O how they cling and wrangle, some who claim
> For preacher and monk the honored name!
> For, quarreling, each to his view they cling.
> Such folk see only one side of a thing."

Coaching for Action: Driving Optimal Performance

The Observer That You Are

1. Choose one challenging situation at work. Make a list of all the actions you are currently taking to work through and handle the situation.
2. Now, go back to the observer models presented in the chapter. Apply the *observer* position to your thinking, and begin a new list by exploring the prism of your perceptions around this challenge. Write down your assumptions, biases, past experiences, and all the factors that are coloring your interpretations as you assign meaning to events within this situation.
3. From this new vantage point, start a third list with new possibilities for actions that can address the situation. What do you notice about each set of actions?

Applying Managerial Mindsets

1. Take the issue from above and apply the five mindsets using worksheet 2-1.
2. How would someone thinking from each mindset address the issue? Which mindsets are strong for you? Which mindsets do you need to develop?

Lagniappe

Your perceptions play a huge role in your success personally and professionally. One very important place where accurate perceptions are vital is in resolving conflicts. Go to our authors' page at www.astd.org/SavvyManager to download Lagniappe 1 to explore how your budding savvy skills will help you better resolve conflicts.

Worksheet 2-1. Developing Managerial Mindsets

1. Think of a current challenge at work. Make some notes about the key facts of the situation and the people involved.

_____

_____

2. Now rethink the same situation from each of the five different mindsets. Make your notes in the space provided.

Reflective Mindset The ability to step back and think about what has happened	
Analytical Mindset The ability to break apart complex concepts	
Worldly Mindset The ability to examine events with a global view	
Collaborative Mindset The ability to work well with a host of others	
Action Mindset The ability to execute effectively	

3. What new ideas have emerged that allow you to think of the situation with new possibilities for action?

_____

_____

Addressing Emotions: The Third Rail of Managing

He who knows others is learned.
He who knows himself is wise.

—Lao Tse

Build your savvy as you learn to

- identify how emotional intelligence links to savvy managing
- take control and effectively leverage your emotional energy
- build awareness of the four quadrants of consciousness
- strengthen workplace relationships by establishing a culture of trust

Emotions are the third rail of managing. It's a fact: Where there are people, there are emotions. We realize that most business books skirt the topic of managing emotions because it ventures into areas that are often considered off limits in the workplace. Emotions are seen as personal and private, and addressing them is difficult and feels uncomfortable. However, handling emotional issues in the workplace is a part of the job faced by every manager. Ignore them at your own peril! Savvy managers know that it is strategically smarter to address emotional issues.

■ ■ ■

Real Time: Bill's Story

When I pledged a fraternity 30 years ago in college, I remember going through "hell week." I thought I'd never go through something as emotionally draining and challenging again. I was wrong! Today ended what I can easily label "hell week" at my plant. It was a week of delivering performance appraisals that were not in keeping with our espoused philosophy of seeing our employees as valuable, contributing partners in our business. As I walk around the plant passing people in the hall, their demeanor exhibits a mood that is not pretty. And it falls to me, as the plant's GM, to help my people recover and move forward.

I can deal with the day-to-day stuff. After all, people can really test one another's patience. We've all been together a long time and know that certain things will trigger high-level emotional outbursts. I honestly think some of my managers "yank my chain" just to get a reaction from me. The issues get addressed, and often we bury the hatchet over a game of pool and a cold one at BJ's.

This is different. Last month, the home office violated the first commandment of management, "Don't mess with people's money." At a time when our stock price is up, production costs are down, and sales look great, management decides to give out minimum raises. They sent out a directive telling us to make sure the words in the formal written reviews matched the lower raises. Talk about changing the spirit of the entire performance review process. I'm sure corporate has sound rationale for this decision, but it's incredibly hard to find it, let alone put an acceptable spin to it.

My managers have spent the week conducting reviews. With each passing day, the mood and energy spiral downward. Trust is shattered, and integrity is being questioned on all fronts. I can appreciate these feelings; receiving my own review from my manager was discouraging. I'm struggling to understand my own emotions and keep my self-talk positive.

I've got the weekend to get my act together. As the GM, I know everyone will be watching me, waiting for me to say something and take some steps to make it right. With integrity being questioned, how will I keep my best people from leaving? How do I reestablish trust? What words can I honestly say that will put this behind us, validate what everyone is experiencing, and begin to regain what we just lost?

■ ■ ■

Think of emotions as the energy that moves you to action, much like gasoline moves your car. Knowing when and at what pressure level to press your emotional gas pedal has ramifications in all aspects of your life. Your coaching in this chapter is all about taking control of your emotional energy. Through reflection and practice, you learn to channel emotional energy in ways that work for you and the people you manage.

We begin the chapter by discussing the contemporary concept of emotional intelligence (EI). Because managing others requires that you first manage yourself, you will see how two elements of emotional intelligence, self-awareness and self-management, link directly to our savvy skill of self-managing. Linked to emotional intelligence and going one level deeper is a conversation about how emotions and moods shape the work environment. We make a critical distinction between mood, which is your every day emotional level, and emotions, which vary and are triggered by some event. These elements are present in all of your communications and interactions. They play an integral role in delivering the results you and your team generate.

Venturing even more deeply into how you show up, we explore the work of philosopher Ken Wilber. The discussion about the quadrants of consciousness exposes some of the underlying reasons behind your choice of actions. We end the chapter with that deeply rooted core value, trust. The mix of these topics, all grounded in the affective (emotional) domain, will shed new light on the interactions happening on a daily basis in your workplace.

The Other Intelligence

Emotional intelligence, a phrase coined by pioneering psychologists Mayer and Salovey in 1990, might simply be defined as allowing your emotions to work for you. EI comprises accurately perceiving emotions in oneself and others, and being able to manage your own emotions. EI connects to your ability to use emotions to facilitate thinking and understanding. Available research supports the idea that connecting from your emotional domain is an even greater indicator of success and achievement than your IQ or "book smarts." This certainly supports our placement of self-managing as your first savvy skill.

> **Skills for Emotional Intelligence**
> - Self-awareness
> - Self-management
> - Motivation
> - Social awareness
> - Relationship management

From the numerous versions available, we submit that EI consists of five developmental components that produce internal emotional balance and social adeptness. EI starts with your ability to recognize and appropriately express your emotions. Emotionally intelligent people know how to motivate themselves to higher levels of personal growth and performance. Fully understanding emotions increases your social graces and helps you feel comfortable interacting with all different kinds of people. It allows you to build and maintain strong working relationships. In this section, we focus in depth on these first two EI building blocks of awareness and management. Strategies about how to build social awareness and create strong relationships are discussed later in the chapter, where we share Wilber's quadrants of consciousness. Motivation, the remaining building block of EI, has chapter 5 all to itself.

Self-awareness is the starting point for developing EI and perhaps the most difficult to explore. At a base level, most people want the same things though not necessarily in the same order or degree. People want to perform meaningful work, to provide for themselves and their families, and to enjoy a good life. Yet just what these things actually mean and how they manifest for you is unique and personal. And it is equally true for every individual in your organization.

Self-awareness demands that you continually observe yourself, monitoring your perceptions and noticing how your thoughts lead to your actions that create your results. As you become more self-aware, you better understand what is important to you and what you want (really, really want). As the fog lifts, you gain clarity about your feelings about events in your personal universe. Being self-aware builds confidence because you understand why you do what you do. Self-awareness means that you recognize your experiences and understand your basic temperament, both of which shape you, but do not exempt your actions.

> *The truth is that our finest moments are most likely to occur when we are feeling deeply uncomfortable, unhappy, or unfulfilled. For it is only in such moments, propelled by our discomfort, that we are likely to step out of our ruts and start searching for different ways or truer answers.*
>
> —M. Scott Peck

It is important that you develop self-awareness, but then what? It certainly is not enough to just say, *Oh yeah, I know those things about myself. That's just how I am!* Emotionally intelligent people take the next step. Self-awareness leads to being authentic, which connects to *self-management*, the next building block of emotional intelligence and our first savvy skill. Managing yourself is about personal discipline, control, and direction. It can be explained by both what you do and don't do. It means that you practice self-control, gaining mastery over what you think, feel, and do. Self-management keeps you centered and moving in your desired direction. It does not

mean that you stifle or suppress your emotions—that you give up feeling. But rather, it allows you to intelligently deal with your thoughts and emotions so that you effectively respond, rather than react to events that happen daily in your life. Self-management means that you hold yourself accountable (Goleman 1998; Weisinger 1998).

> *You cannot make yourself feel something you do not feel, but you can make yourself do right in spite of your feelings.*
> —Pearl S. Buck

As you will see from the two examples that follow, the practice of self-management is not just about managing negative behaviors but also about making sure that positive intentions are well placed. Take a look at how Adam and Rick are incorporating coaching on the job into their unique learning challenges.

Adam is a high-energy, very proactive bank branch manager. He shows up as a "rah-rah" cheerleader, using superlatives and bold directives, hoping to enhance performances and results for this branch. For many on his staff, he appears phony and superficial, just too much! Although they appreciate his positive approach, they want him to be more genuine and better grounded. Adam is aware of how he is showing up to his staff. What he is learning to do is to ratchet down his intensity a few notches. He is working to better manage his positive energy at a level to which his staff will respond, one that helps them achieve greater performance and results.

Working on an oil drilling platform is a high-stress and dangerous job. As a drilling supervisor, Rick was known for his temper. He had the infamous reputation for kicking his hard hat across the drilling platform floor during conflicts and high stress events. Talk about having an adult temper tantrum! Then Rick developed his self-managing skills and discovered a better technique for handling his frustration and anger. Now, as a rig manager, his temper manifests as a quiet, tense moment. It's a message his staff has learned to read and appreciate. Through awareness and practice, Rick has found more appropriate and effective ways to handle his emotions during challenging situations.

Your coaching here asks you to recognize the impact that your emotions have within you, and what they do to those you manage. Stop. Take a breath. Learn to appreciate that your first thought might trigger more of a knee-jerk reaction than an effective response. As you grow emotionally, you will learn to respond in ways that offer better alternatives for everyone. You will find your greatest feats as a manager occur when you align your thinking with your emotions and take action from that centered place.

 Savvy Translation: Savvy managers grow their emotional intelligence. They take their emotional temperature before taking action. They self-manage to ensure that they respond to events in ways that harness positive emotional energy.

Emotions and Moods at Work

Believe it or not, you have a choice about how you experience everything in your life. The invisible roots of that choice are embedded in your moods and emotions, two distinctive elements that dictate how you show up in your world on a daily basis. Moods and emotions are both energy fields from which you take action. Emotionally intelligent people understand the distinctions and use these powerful energies to great advantage.

> *Happiness is when what you think, what you say, and what you do are in harmony.*
> —Mohandas Gandhi

Emotions are strong feelings that are triggered by some event or circumstance. Someone cuts you off on the highway and you might feel angry, irritated, or scared. You may feel excited, overjoyed, or humbled when receiving a standing ovation after giving a speech. Emotions are experienced as totally subjective responses to both pleasant and unpleasant events within a certain context. Eventually, most every emotion will fade, being replaced with another emotion from a new situation or circumstance. Emotions are fleeting and have been likened at times to a roller coaster ride!

Follow along with this example to see how your emotional brain and your thinking brain frame events and move you to respond to those events: Chris receives the promotion that you thought would be yours. Enter your emotional brain. What are you feeling? Words that might describe your feelings in this moment could include disappointed, ticked off, furious, jealous, angry, frustrated, miffed, resentful, or confused. The feelings that emerge are separate from what you might be thinking. You might be thinking that Chris is competent, qualified, and has more experience. You might also be thinking that your boss forgot to consider your longer company tenure and greater flexibility for travel with the job. Although you know why Chris was chosen, and you think Chris deserves the promotion, you feel it should have been yours.

The thinking and emotional brains are having an argument inside your head. The more emotionally intelligent you are, the more capable you are in assessing and aligning these two powerful forces. You learn to shift your emotions to a place from which you can take conscious, effective action. Getting control of your emotions and using them to reason and validate your thoughts are key. This emotionally intelligent behavior taps into your savvy skills of self-managing, reflecting, and acting consciously—preparing you to vie for a promotion the next time.

Your mood, conversely, is how you normally present yourself. Think about people you know. Someone may come to mind as a person who is always happy and upbeat, resilient to whatever is happening in his or her life. Or you might picture someone who is negative and seems to always be down. It's the classic "glass half empty/half full" scenario. Some people experience everyday life with an outlook toward possibilities. Others stay focused on the gloom and doom of life. Although your moods can vary somewhat whether you are at home or work, there is an undercurrent that manifests fairly consistently. Table 3-1 highlights the distinctions between emotions and moods.

To develop strategies that effectively manage emotions and moods, you must first recognize the mood or emotional field that is coloring your world and controlling your actions. You must give it a name and consciously choose to manage its affect.

Table 3-1. Emotions and Moods

Emotions	Moods
Usually triggered by an event or situation	A way of being tuned into the world
Both learned and biological responses	Often transparent
Have energy that capture you and take control	How you show up
Control the expression of your emotional reaction to a trigger	Shape your future
Come before the language you use to express your feelings	Determine your range of available actions
	Open and close possibilities
	How you engage and ground your relationships with others

Source: Adapted from Newfield Network, Inc.

You must acknowledge how your feelings power actions that produce outcomes. You must reflect to discern if what you are feeling is serving the outcome you want. If it is, then your emotions and mood are likely aligned with your thoughts and actions. If they are not, then you must work through the emotional issue at hand and choose new emotions that better support the results you want.

> *Before you can inspire with emotion, you must be swamped with it yourself. Before you can move their tears, your own must flow. To convince them, you must yourself believe.*
>
> —Winston Churchill

Embracing a mood and emotional energy, one that helps you achieve what you want in both your career and personal life, is hard. It takes practice and lots of reflective, inner dialogue to sort through what is happening and then consciously choose to feel differently. You cannot control what happens to you, but you can always control your reactions and responses. No one can ever make you feel a certain way. You choose how you show up outwardly. You are accountable for that.

As the manager, make your mood attractive to recruit others like yourself to your team. Be sensitive and receptive in coaching your staff as they deal with their inner struggles to align their own conversations. Your ultimate goal is to create workplace harmony that harnesses all the positive emotional energy from yourself and your team.

 Savvy Translation: Savvy managers appreciate and respect the power of the emotional domain in producing results. First, they choose their own emotions and embrace a mood that works for them. Then they work to harness the emotional energy of their workforce, steering it in positive ways.

Quadrants of Consciousness

Your role as manager demands that you interact with lots of people to produce the results that you really want. You need to build strong strategic relationships throughout your organization and with customers and vendors. The strategic relationship competency connects to the last two EI skills: social awareness and relationship management. These skills focus on the often transparent roots of human interactions and include elements such as awareness, empathy, influence, and collaborative efforts. Your performance is a result of layer upon layer of experiences, both positive and negative, that emerge from interactions with others. Your coaching goal is to increase your understanding of the infinite combinations and complexities embedded in human behaviors to create stronger, more effective relationships with everyone you serve.

Ken Wilber, a modern philosopher, provides great insight through what he has identified as four quadrants of consciousness, which are shown in table 3-2. The four quadrants are the internal/individual, internal/collective, external/individual and external/collective (Wilber 1996). What you are seeing are distinctions in how you filter or perceive what is happening in your world within each quadrant. Stick with our discussion as the quadrants of consciousness reveal blind spots that guide your actions. Because many of your actions stem from these levels of consciousness, your understanding here will further sharpen your skills for managing yourself and others.

Look at the internal/individual (I/I) quadrant in table 3-2. This is your "I" place, where you are self-aware. It is where your values, opinions, and beliefs live. Your I/I quadrant is the place where you conduct internal conversations and set your intentions. *I choose to go to school in the hope of expanding my career opportunities* might be an "I" conversation. The I/I quadrant also reveals how you hold yourself in relation to the world outside. *I'm terrible at math* or *I'm shy* are two internal conversations that might happen for you within the I/I quadrant. Clearly, your belief that you are terrible at math or shy could have major ramifications on the types of jobs you consider and your earning potential throughout your career. Because "I" conversations can be invisible, one of your first challenges is to reflect on your own "I" conversation. *What is it that you believe to be true about you? How do you hold yourself?*

Table 3-2. Quadrants of Consciousness

	Internal				External
Individual	Personal beliefs Personal values Stories held as true Intentions Opinions Internal talk		**"I"**	**"It"**	Conversations with others Observable behaviors Actions Spoken requests Results achieved Commitments made
Collective	Traditions Historical story Social norms Shared values Worldviews	**"We"**		**"Its"**	Institutions Policies, rules Structure Societal views Technology/tools

Source: Wilber (1996). Used by permission.

> *Insight, I believe, refers to the depth of understanding that comes by setting experiences, yours and mine, familiar and exotic, new and old, side by side, learning by letting them speak to one another.*
>
> —Mary Catherine Bateson

The internal/collective (I/C) quadrant in table 3-2 speaks to the "We." This quadrant acknowledges your origins; roots; traditions; and the shared worldviews, values, and beliefs of the cultural group into which you are born or have chosen to join. You might internally/collectively speak as an American citizen, a southerner, or a New Yorker, or as someone with Spanish, Italian, or Cajun-French heritage. Think about your own cultural roots and family traditions. The "We" explains your social thinking about key issues. I/C thinking often goes unchallenged, especially under the umbrella of political correctness. *Can you identify some of your "We" conversations?*

The external/individual (E/I) quadrant in table 3-2 addresses actions within the framework of the objective world outside yourself. "It" speaks to the behaviors set by others, which you must follow in specific situations. Current "It" conversations include some of the established norms at your workplace: the dress code, shaking hands, open door policies, customer service behaviors, phone etiquette. Think of the norms and acceptable behaviors at your company. *What are the "It" conversations that guide policy decisions where you work?*

Finally, the external/collective (E/C) quadrant in table 3-2 examines the large societal and institutional rules that serve to inform a particular worldview. The political climate and social attitudes, along with advances in technology, direct your "Its" conversations. For example, in the 1950s and 1960s the worldview for girls was that they become teachers, nurses, or secretaries; then they get married and stay home to raise their families. Husbands were to be the breadwinners. There was a time when men stood up when ladies entered the room and executives had private dining rooms and washrooms. *What has changed and what has stayed the same for different societies throughout the world today?*

These four quadrants of consciousness unlock a higher level of capability for collaborative action. When applied in your organization, they generate greater coordinated performance for all employees. With the increased level of diversity in the workforce, your understanding of what the quadrants suggest becomes even more critical. Here, we offer two examples to clarify the concept of consciousness and the important role it plays in your evolving into a savvy manager.

Rosa comes from a culture that teaches women to be silent. As her manager, you have stressed the point that you want her to ask questions whenever she doesn't understand. Because she asks no questions, you assume that she understands her job duties and responsibilities. Later, when she does not complete a task correctly, you demand to know why she did not ask for help.

> *Nobody goes to work*
> *to do a bad job.*
> —W. Edwards Deming

Being savvier here, you might have reflected upon her "We" internal/collective quadrant. Even without realizing how deeply her cultural traditions were embedded, part of your managerial initiative should have been to check with her during the performance phases of her work. A simple request for an update or brainstorming conversation would have revealed her dilemma. Taking this example a step further, most people do not ask for help because our American external/collective quadrant has taught us that asking for help is a sign of weakness. Even though nothing could be further from the truth, asking for help still remains a huge hurdle for many people.

Gene comes from a military background and is accustomed to people doing what they are told to do. He likes to give directions without interruption and expects his team to just go do it. His team of Generation Xers is frustrated, to say the least. Gene's directives are strong and leave little room for alternative points of view or discussion. His staff wants the opportunity to brainstorm and be part of the planning. They say that he doesn't even know their names or what they do on the job. He definitely comes to his job from the external/individual quadrant, the "It" conversation.

The old adage "Knowledge is power" applies here. When you begin to peel back the layers of transparent thought that lead to your actions, you reveal interesting phenomena around why you and other people take certain actions. Discerning the deeper roots of human behavior offers you new action possibilities for managing relationships in the workplace. Recognize how deeply ingrained these quadrants of consciousness may be for you in your present position. Your savvy skills soar as you identify your own conversations at each of the four quadrants. As you become more conscious of just which conversation is directing your actions, you improve your social awareness and the understanding of all around you. This increased knowledge becomes truly powerful to maintain relationships in an unpredictable marketplace in constant flux. The wisdom you gain helps you coordinate the actions among your team to increase performance and produce greater results.

Savvy Translation: Savvy managers know that performance is linked to the "I," "We," "It," and "Its" quadrants of consciousness. They recognize that these are deeply embedded and transparent. They fearlessly enter the emotional domain to both validate others and illuminate new possibilities.

Trust: Your "Character" Conversation

Our efforts to help you better understand and manage emotions in the workplace conclude with coaching on the topic of trust. The bedrock of all relationships, trust flows from the personal, *I will love you forever*, to the workplace, *I'll get the project to you by noon tomorrow*. Trust enables commitment. Whether you trust someone or not is a decision based on your own personal nature and your experiences with that person. You may be very trusting and trustworthy by your own inclinations. Or you may be less trusting and more guarded. You create your own trust dynamic through your words, actions, and commitments. There is a certain vulnerability to trust, because its alter ego, distrust, is an ever-present possibility.

Although organizations can survive without trust, few will really thrive. Trust is the transparent fiber that builds the networks within which relationships between individuals and among teams are established and maintained. It creates an invisible sense of community, enabling people to work together comfortably and productively. Again, it is all about you as a manager and team member, developing competencies to become trustworthy and to foster trusting relationships in your organization. When your employees see their leadership acting in authentic ways, trust will permeate the company. When the actions of the leadership strain the trust commentary, employees will lapse into a self-protective mode. Reestablishing trust with employees requires significant time, attention, and authenticity.

We distinguish trust as telling the truth, your truth, even when it is a difficult thing to do. It is a choice you make, action you take. Within the framework of a relationship, trust is built through small steps over time that happen through honest interactions. Trust is a way of being: trustworthy and genuine. It lives in your ability to give your word, make promises, and have full accountability to follow through on your commitments. Trust means that when someone is depending upon you, you deliver as promised, or you renegotiate the promise (Olalla 2000).

> *A man who doesn't trust himself can never really trust anyone else.*
> —Cardinal de Retz

Trust is never about a technique; nor is it automatic. It is not a given but something that is earned through mutually satisfying dealings that are part of social interactions and relationship building. The word that takes center stage when talking about trust is integrity. Integrity epitomizes the cliché "walking your talk." It is your alignment as a whole person, in thought, word, and deed. It means doing the right thing, even when no one is watching. Trust is a conversation about your character, individually and collectively.

Elements of Trust

Consider these three examples of situations where trust is established. Once plans are determined and agreed on, you trust that your network administrator will complete her specific portion of your project. You trust that a friend, who has indicated that he will help you box items and haul furniture to your new apartment, is actually going to arrive on moving day at the agreed-upon time and be ready to work. You trust that your babysitter will aptly (if not lovingly) take care of your child when you go out to dinner. However, in each of these cases, you would not trust any of these people to perform open-heart surgery on you!

Four elements of trust—sincerity, reliability, competence, and involvement—are applied when placing your trust in another (Sieler 2003). Each of the scenarios above points directly to one of these elements. These elements play a vital role whenever you assess your own level of trustworthiness, and when making assessments about members of your team. Table 3-3 defines the elements of trust that can help you direct your thought processes. As your coaches, we challenge you to master these elements in your own life and to then model them to help others embody trust on the job.

Table 3-3. Elements of Trust

Element	Definition	Coaching Questions
Sincerity	Genuine Pure agenda Real	Am I genuine? Do my words reflect what I really feel and say about things that affect me and others? How am I showing up?
Reliability	Predictability Certainty	Do I deliver the results I commit to deliver in a consistent manner? Is my best the standard of measure I use?
Competence	Skills Abilities	Are my skills and abilities fully developed? What more do I need to develop to reach my full potential?
Involvement	Connection Validation	How well do I integrate myself with others? Am I empathetic? Do I understand their concerns and do they understand mine? Am I seeing the whole picture?

Source: Adapted from Newfield Network, Inc.

As these elements of trust converge, you can better understand how relevant actions become in deciding whether a person is judged trustworthy. For purposes of discussion, let's say that you are the department manager. You ask Joe to assist you in taking inventory. At this point, you have made a conscious assessment that Joe is competent for this task. He seems to be a sincere, hard worker. You know from past experiences that if he says he will be there, he will show up, because he is very reliable. Finally, because of previous conversations and interactions with him, you know that he appreciates just how important the inventory is to you and the organization. All this happens, somewhat transparently, and weaves the framework of the relationship that exists between you and Joe.

> *Few things help an individual more than to place responsibility upon him, and to let him know that you trust him.*
>
> —Booker T. Washington

Because this task is above and beyond what he usually does, Joe has the option to say "yes" or "no" to doing the task. He commits, shows up on time, and assists in a manner that supports your previous assessment of him. When this happens, the trust relationship is strengthened. However, if Joe does not show up and, furthermore, does not call with a valid reason, you begin to question both his reliability and sincerity and the relationship becomes shaky. If Joe shows up with a hangover from partying the night before, totally inept for the task at hand, his competence and reliability come into question. If he does not show up and does not call, his lack of sincerity is validated. All these assessments, made by you and others who witness Joe's actions, link to his trustworthiness. They establish the foundation for future actions and the working relationship between you and Joe.

Strategies for Building Trust

No manager really has the time to deal with employees who cannot be trusted. The strategies that follow are coaching that furthers your own development in the arena of trust. Evaluate your effectiveness as you apply these strategies in your workplace. Make changes as needed:

- Hire people who are trustworthy. Look for employees who are capable of forming strong working relationships. Invest the time to hire the right person. Don't settle! Hire talent, not just bodies.
- Always speak the truth to your staff. Divulge all that you can comfortably tell. When you cannot share certain information, say so. Remember

that in the absence of information, people assume the worst. Don't lie!

- Practice integrity where your words always equal your actions. Become the model of exactly what you want to see. Speak up and take decisive actions when trust is violated. Don't allow mistrust to fester.

- Keep confidences! Listen attentively to employees. Validate and honor their concerns. Treat people with dignity and respect. Don't gossip.

The Bottom Line: Addressing Emotions—The Third Rail of Managing

The chapter's themes of emotional intelligence, moods and emotions, levels of consciousness, and trust share familiar concepts with fresh insights. Some of them may be very foreign to you. We congratulate you for having the tenacity to persevere to the end. It takes courage to really look inside and discover your real self, warts and all! It is all part of evolving. This means that you know more about yourself than anyone else does. You are learning to make your emotions work for you. Gaining more understanding about your moods and emotions puts you in control of making decisions and taking effective conscious action.

Higher emotional intelligence allows you to show up as a genuine, effective, and real person with one "face" that all can see. It produces that difficult-to-put-your-finger-on way about you, which can be summed up in one word: integrity. Real alignment of your words, emotions, and actions builds trust through your own trustworthy actions. While you speak your truth, you must also hear the truth of others. Strong relationships are founded on trust and built one step at a time. And when trust is challenged or lost, difficult issues must be addressed for it to be reestablished.

What we have suggested must seem like a utopian vision for being more open and honest with your employees and co-workers. However, we fully realize that the complex issues and competing challenges facing managers often prevent the level of openness and honesty that we have proposed. Work the vision to make it as viable as possible in your organization. Take appropriate action to reconcile interpersonal issues. Find your courage and address those emotionally charged situations and problems. It is so much better to handle them then to ignore them, hoping they will just go away. Trust us! They seldom do. Unreconciled emotional issues fester and build resentment. It is better to get things out in the open and know which emotional elements need to be addressed. The next chapter offers models for change and tools to help you in this regard.

Use It or Lose It

Write down the one key idea that you "got" as a takeaway from your reading. Then write down what you plan to do starting tomorrow to integrate this idea, practice it, and make it a habit.

1. What I got. _____

   _____

2. How I will use it tomorrow. _____

   _____

3. Which savvy skill(s) I am developing. _____

   _____

Reflection Interval

The short poem that follows should be a great reminder. Do you truly know yourself? What do you feel when you look yourself in the eye? Work to build your own strength of character and self-confidence as you grow your savvy skills.

The Guy in the Glass
By Dale Wimbrow—copyright 1934; used with permission

When you get what you want in your struggle for self
and the world makes you king for a day.
Just go to a mirror and look at yourself
and see what that man has to say.
For it isn't your father, your mother, or wife
whose judgment upon you must pass.
The fellow whose verdict counts most in your life,
is the one staring back from the glass.
Some people may think you a straight-shootin' chum
and call you a wonderful guy,
but the man in the glass says you're only a bum—
if you can't look him straight in the eye.
He's the fellow to please—never mind all the rest,
for he's with you clear up to the end.
And you've passed your most dangerous, difficult test
if the man in the glass is your friend.
You may fool the whole world down the pathway of life
and get pats on your back as you pass,
but your final reward will be heartaches and tears—
if you've cheated the man in the glass.

Coaching for Action: Driving Optimal Performance
Developing Your Emotional Intelligence

1. What do you know about yourself? Make a list of all the things you truly believe about yourself. Ask a trusted colleague or your significant other to give you feedback.

2. What do you need to better manage your performance at work? How much more effective could you be if you showed up differently? What would that different person look like? Formulate an action plan with strategies for new actions, something from which you might realize results in the next three months.

Building Trusting Relationships

Relationships are never static. They take effort and attention to keep them productive and satisfying for all persons involved.

1. Make a list of important strategic relationships on the job. Now, identify the emotions or moods that you attach to these relationships. What relationships need improvement or rejuvenation? What strategies can you use to shore up these relationships?

2. Which of the strategies suggested in the subsection "Strategies for Building Trust" do you currently practice? Which might you add as part of your building stronger work relationships?

Lagniappe

Your moods and emotions come with you to work every day. Use the exercise "Mood Revealed" in Lagniappe 2 at www.astd.org/SavvyManager to help you understand how emotions and moods may be affecting you on the job. Think of a specific situation and complete the worksheet you can download from the website.

Embracing Change

Not everything that is faced can be changed,
but nothing can be changed until it is faced.

—James Baldwin

Build your savvy as you learn to

- become a *change avatar* in your organization
- maneuver skillfully through the sustainable change process
- use reflection to consciously embrace change
- develop skills to lead the charge for organizational change

Change is all around us. It's the one, sure constant in our lives! The common cliché, that everyone hates change, has given way to the honest reality that change is the very essence of what happens on a daily basis. Nothing stays the same. Forces that had little, if any, impact on the businesses of your grandfathers and maybe even your parents, are now driving American businesses, albeit sometimes to distraction! In 1988, the management consultant Tom Peters asked us to reconsider the old adage, "If it ain't broke, don't fix it," proposing instead, "If it ain't broke, you haven't looked hard enough. Fix it anyway" (Peters 1988, 3). He amended his comments in 2003, predicting that "anything is possible. Anything is *likely*. Are you ready? Change is coming and coming fast" (Peters 2003, 57).

■ ■ ■

Real Time: Connie's Story

Every day I walk in here there is something new to handle. If it's not a new product, it's additional services offered on old products. Last week it was all new procedures to learn to access our databases. Crisis management lives! As the director of customer relations, I am constantly putting out fires. My people are frustrated to the point of cynicism, which is not good. Everyone is so negative. Every proposed solution is wrong, and people are unwilling to even try. My bigger challenge is trying to keep this attitude from showing itself to customers.

The new system was supposed to be user friendly and make accessing and processing all sorts of information much faster and more efficient. Customers would be able to get product information, their service agreement information, and technical support online without actually speaking with a real live human being, making some form of help available 24/7. The new software would free up service center personnel to work with new customers and new products and to handle more complex problems. So much for intentions!

These "best-laid plans" are not exactly working as planned. Whoever sold us this software promised a simple, smooth transition. Seems like the only thing smooth was his sales pitch! We ditched the old system totally and now we have to clean up the mess. We look foolish when we try to explain to our customers about online procedures that aren't working yet, for them or us. Training has been a slow, complicated process. We've got to get it together to meet customer expectations with the same service excellence we promise and used to deliver.

As difficult as we have it, it's worse for the IT team. They get frustrated end users wanting everything to be fixed yesterday! Fortunately, the people in IT have mastered some key people skills and are a flexible, responsive group. They just take all the changes in stride. At the last place I worked, the systems guys were overworked, and their horrendous people skills made everything worse.

Surviving and managing through all these changes is the real task before me! As a team, we need to process these changes and take time on the learning curve to do it right. I need to get my people to stop growling at each other and start seeing what they need to do. We all know this won't be the last change coming our way. What can I do differently so that we perform in a way that makes all of this change appear seamless?

■ ■ ■

The pressure of constant change is your silent partner in business—sometimes obvious, other times quite elusive. The phenomenon labeled as change drives every individual to question what to do about it: embrace it or fight it? With these choices in mind, your coaching about change becomes twofold. First, we want you to focus on your own ability to adapt to new circumstances. This directly links to your growing self-awareness and ability to self-manage. As you discover how you respond or react to changes, you become more capable and the transition from old to new becomes smoothly folded into your routine.

The second point addresses your managerial ability to encourage and support each member of your team during the chaos, confusion, and emotional upheaval of a change process. We want you to take a deeper look at just how system or process changes in your organization have an impact on the interactions and relationships of the people involved in the change. Your role must move beyond that of change agent to *change avatar*, which we define as someone who embodies a keen insightfulness and the ability to recognize the nuances that are revealed in all three domains (language, emotion, and body) of the L-E-B Model (see chapter 1).

With a higher level of wisdom as change avatar, you realize the emotional spiral that major changes produce. This is especially true for the workplace changes that have dramatic ramifications on the personal lives of your employees. As a change avatar, you know the right words to say and what approach to take with each employee as he or she moves through the dynamics of the change initiative. Your highly developed observer skills help you monitor behavioral signs that show alignment or reveal struggle. Developing the wisdom of the avatar grows directly from your capacity to learn and apply the savvy skills.

> *We are often trapped by the images we hold of ourselves.*
> —Gareth Morgan

Sustainable Change

Rarely do you move through a day without experiencing some type of change. Every change you encounter requires a shift in your thinking, and your increased awareness of how you think is the focus of our coaching. The greater the change and the more it affects you at a core level, the more you will have to shift your thoughts, address any accompanying emotions, and steady your course of action. A change in the color of paper or ink used on invoices might only give you a momentary pause. However, revamping departments and shifting personnel will require more reflection and adjustment. Though you might agree conceptually and see the value of a new process, restructuring plan, or business strategy, leaving the comfort of what you know and do well is difficult. Changes, even those you truly desire and embrace, tug at your emotions and your physical well-being.

Sustainable change is change that endures. It roots itself deeply into your core, causing what was once new to become a familiar and comfortable habit. Sustainable change restores stability and balance around new actions, beliefs, or ideas. Reaching that place of balance (from a fleeting variance to a long-term, sustainable change) requires the cohesion and alignment of language (thoughts), emotions (feelings) and body (physical). Once sustained, these new actions and processes become the platform from which future changes will take shape. It's continuous process improvement theory put to the test every day. Nothing lasts forever.

> *The first problem for all of us, men and women, is not to learn, but to unlearn.*
>
> —Gloria Steinem

Your Story Rules!

You know the cliché "It's my story and I'm sticking to it." Your personal story, how you see yourself, plays a prominent role in how you handle change. It informs what you can and cannot do. Your unique story is a product of the mental messages, images, and perceptions that you hold about who you are (smart or dumb), how you behave (extrovert or shy), and all that is possible for you (everything or nothing). Stop now and consider your own thoughts as you have been reading. What are you thinking, especially when you may not agree with a point we are making? Right now, your story is supporting or inhibiting your efforts to embrace our coaching suggestions about your savvy skill development.

Change disrupts your story. Yesterday, you were the director of creative advertising; today, you are offered an early retirement package. Yesterday, you were an assistant manager; today, you get promoted to products manager of a new team. Yesterday, you were a competent employee of the XYZ company; today, restructuring leaves you unemployed. For the past two years, you had an office with a window; today, your workspace in the new building is a center cubicle. Yesterday, you processed reports the way you always did; today, you've got new software to learn. Yesterday, you worked for the ABC company; today, an announcement says that your biggest competitor is acquiring you.

How you cope with each of these kinds of changes, and the many others that could be mentioned here, is a function of how you cling to your story. Fostering sustainable change requires you to examine your personal story. This is also where your roles of manager and of change avatar mesh. You work with employees, helping them assess and reframe their stories so that they fit into the new realities of your changing workplace.

A Walk Through the Process

Look at figure 4-1. The model depicts the sustainable change process. Follow along as we guide you through the steps. The process starts with you in balance, comfortable with how things are. Then something occurs, and your story gets jolted. The significance of any event determines what happens next. If the event requires a minor change, you move easily through it with only slight adjustments. If it is a major change, the event will trigger your emotions to a higher degree. During your emotional turmoil, you will feel uncertain and out of balance and experience disrupted thoughts, conflicting inner dialogue, anger, and frustration. Some people get stuck in this place, labeled as a "reactive loop," and never fully adjust to the change. This might be due to their discomfort with the change, fear of loss, or resentment. This downward cycle intensifies with each iteration and becomes a place where some people spend their whole lives.

> *What is necessary to change a person is to change his awareness of himself.*
> —Abraham Maslow

Your alternate path is to choose a response that helps you to embrace the change, as represented by the "responsive track" shown in figure 4-1. You engage all your savvy skills. You reflect and assess the emotional triggers being energized by the new requirements. You self-manage and control impulsive energy that does not really serve you, your team, or the situation at hand. You respond deliberately, without reacting, which opens your internal action generation center. You reflect further on options and the outcomes that might be possible from each one. You expand your thinking using models like the five mindsets or "ladder of inference" to explore what is happening, as well as what is needed, from different vantage points and through a variety of filters. You act consciously as thoughts and ideas move from possibilities to conception to execution. You transform yourself, building a new story and image around the change that puts you back in balance. Your results are sustainable change.

Figure 4-1. The Sustainable Change Process

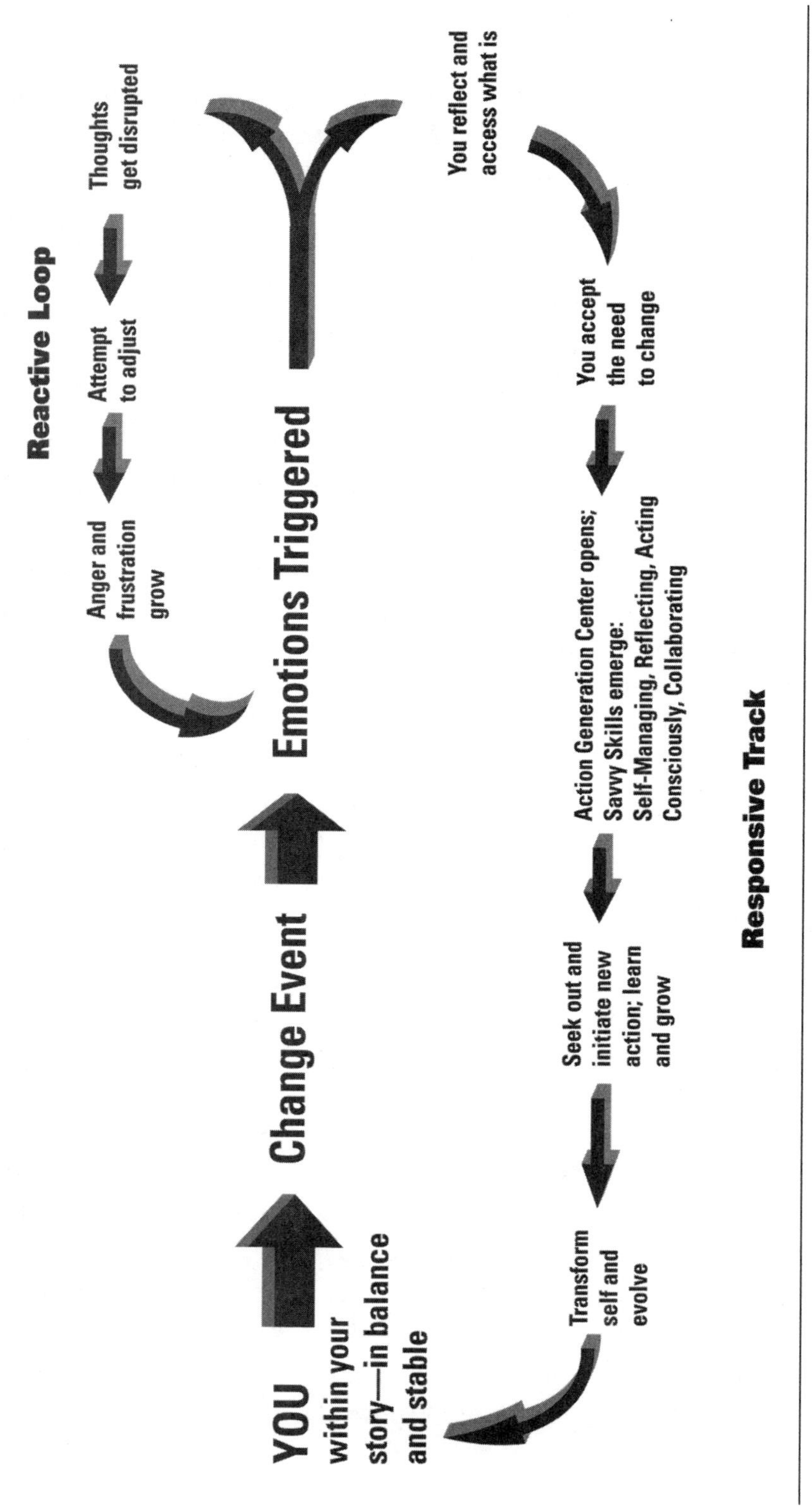

Moving from the abstract to a concrete example, this familiar scenario will help you visualize just how you cycle through the sustainable change process. You decide it's time to get healthy. You make the commitment to eat right (avoiding lots of foods you love), exercise (something you hate), and stop smoking and/or drinking excessively. The first few days go well. You are clearly focused on achieving your goal. Somewhere around the third or fourth day, temptation shows up. You feel that first pressure and uncertainty from the dark side. Your muscles are sore from your workouts, and your cravings for chocolate or a cigarette are hitting you hard. Your emotions are whirling!

Can you stay with the plan? If you do, new habits supporting good health will be yours from the changes you are making. If you revert to old behaviors, any future attempt to change will be that much harder. You tough it out. Slowly, the changes in your routine begin to produce visible results. Biceps are revealed and you can finally zip those jeans. You feel and look better and have more energy. Your new eating habits mean "one piece of chocolate" is just one piece of chocolate! Even if you should fall

back, revert to an old habit, you just don't enjoy it as much. You can feel the rub against the new pattern of your health-conscious ways. When this happens, you are headed toward sustaining a healthier lifestyle and a new story about yourself as a health-conscious person.

> *It takes a lot of courage to release the familiar and seemingly secure, to embrace the new.*
>
> —Alan Cohen

Whenever new processes and procedures of some change start creating an emotional minefield, remember this model of sustainable change. Apply it to the complex changes showing up in your workplace. Check right now to see if you are indeed stuck in the reactive loop with some change that is happening in your life. Your growth depends on your ability to flex, to move along the path of responsiveness and transition. Evolve! Shed your old story for new stories that allow you to grow.

We coach our clients to understand that sustainable change is an inside job, especially when they voice wishes about *the company* changing. These are usually yearnings associated with acts of service, courtesy, or effectiveness. What is important to realize is that a company can't make these types of changes unless and until the people within it change—until individuals change. When each person is waiting for someone else to change, it creates somewhat of a vicious cycle, a "catch-22."

Here is our solution, a simple answer that breaks the cycle: To change something within your company, identify the desired change and then simply do it. For example, if you want people to be more courteous, then be courteous. Do you want your company to provide clients with better-quality products and better service? Become known for your own excellent customer service. Make a commitment that every project on which you work will represent your best work, regardless of what anyone else does. It's contagious! Remember, any change starts with you. You make it happen.

 Savvy Translation: Savvy managers know that embracing change requires thinking differently. They learn to self-manage the emotional hooks embedded around a particular event. They take conscious actions and execute every next step as a means to bring themselves back into balance with each change initiative. They model the process they want to see from others.

Consciously Embracing Change

Now that sustainable change is more clearly established for you, *how do you actually make it happen?* We start with the example of Kelly, an engineer who was promoted to manager of his group. This change in roles disrupted his story of himself as "one of the guys," a team player, and qualified field worker. Holding on to his story caused confusion for his team because his inconsistent actions were not meshing with their expectations of what a *manager* should do. Through coaching, he began to see a new story for himself with the twist of himself as a leader, manager, and team player. He recognized how not letting go of his old story was sabotaging his effectiveness. He found a new way to be "one of the guys" that did not compromise his new role as manager.

> *I create the potential for everything else to change when I shift my interpretation of my experience.*
> —David A. Schmaltz

Suppose Kelly had been unable to recognize what he needed to do differently to make the transition from worker to manager. What would have happened if he had gossiped with his staff or started acting as if he was superior to his former peers? Without fully appreciating all the challenges of his new roles and responsibilities, he could have easily derailed. Coaching helped him develop a new story that allowed him to maintain valued friendships with his team members and still command the respect due him as the new manager of the group. Kelly's transition from peer to manager of his team was not an easy shift for him. And yet we ask you to consider that there is a little bit of Kelly in all of us.

What we find from our clients is that it proves helpful to have a clear, systematic process for embracing the conflicting emotions and actions around the rather abstract concept of change. We summarize this process in table 4-1. In transforming changes into new thoughts, actions, and behaviors, you must never lose sight of the emotional component. As you read the explanation for each of the steps below, consider how they can serve you in implementing any changes you may be facing. Notice how your ability to reflect is critically important to your movement through change. Ask yourself those tough questions regarding your own ability for each step.

Table 4-1. Model for Consciously Embracing Change

Step	Actions to Take	Questions to Ask
Letting go	Let go of your old story and past beliefs! Stop old patterns of behavior.	What has a hold on you? What's preventing you from letting go?
Reflecting	*Reflection gives you 20/20 sight. Carve out time to think. Align your L-E-B circles (see figure 1-1). Uncover what is not immediately clear. Articulate the obstacles and your interpretations.*	*What is making you struggle? What is your next step in letting go?*
Experimenting	Fight the fear! Take that calculated risk. Consciously connect to your beginner's mind, opening yourself to new possibilities.	Are you prepared to make mistakes, sometimes lots of them? Knowing that mistakes are part of the experimenting process, can you stay focused and work through them?
Reflecting	*Your 20/20 sight grows. With each experiment, notice how your behaviors have or have not produced the results you want.*	*Are you aligned in thoughts, feelings, and actions? Are your L-E-B circles moving closer together, empowering your actions? Or are your L-E-B circles separating, diminishing your capability to transform and change?*
Integrating	Choose those actions producing the results you want and work to make them new habits. Practice! Integration requires repetition to synthesize skills and apply them effectively.	Do you have the courage to make your new behaviors part of your life? Are you really committed to these new actions? Is your conscious attention focused on this new direction?
Reflecting	*Reflect now at a higher level of consciousness about your new behaviors.*	*Which behaviors are serving you and which require further tweaking? Are you where you want to be?*
Sustaining the change	You are allowing your savvy skills of self-managing, acting consciously, and reflecting to work together to increase your personal capability to move to a new way of taking action. With your change fully embodied, you drive your performance to higher levels.	Are you able to rewrite your story around the new changes? Have your new actions been accomplished with minimum struggle? How are you evolving?

Adopting new habits requires all your savvy skills working together in seamless harmony. Developing the habits of change doesn't always occur through smooth transitions. Courage is required to take that first step. You must become a strong observer and objectively examine your story. You live the change, sometimes just moment by moment, until it becomes who you are—it is embodied in your thoughts, emotions, and behaviors. It's much like this old saying "How do you eat an elephant? One bite at a time!"

Savvy Translation: Savvy managers own their own change process. They are quick to identify filters, uncover barriers, and consciously choose new actions. They are courageous about experimenting to find balance and comfort in the newness.

Leading Organizational Change

When we speak of organizational change, we are really focused on the efforts of the people within your organization. Organizational change can be defined as a synergistic emergence to a new playing field, one requiring different actions and a fresh perspective with new thoughts and greater awareness. Simply, it's all about everyone "being on the same page." Individual efforts are brought together, aligned and then manifest as new actions or beliefs and new habits.

Your role as a manager requires you to champion the change that the company wants to initiate, regardless of your own level of agreement about what is happening. Your ability to be a change avatar plays a vital role here. It takes keen insight about the realities of your workplace culture and environment, as well as your employees, to accomplish changes with minimum commotion and disruption. We've isolated several key strategies and techniques to help you lead the charge in any organizational change initiative. As usual, our concentration is on relationships and personal capacities around change.

Leading the charge for change initiatives demands focus and direction. Think of an aircraft carrier—in changing direction, these huge ships take miles of ocean. They continue to move ahead, just as your organization would continue conducting its daily business while incorporating any change. They alter the direction of their forward motion in small measures to get to the final course setting necessary to arrive at their destination.

> *As we change the way we are in the world, we change the world we are in.*
>
> —Dee Hock

This is the essence of smooth, focused change. The same is true for you and your team. Special efforts are needed to align the endeavors of many into a concerted initiative that supports any organizational change.

Your leadership and avatar wisdom are the starting point for any change initiative. Your role is to present the change plan in a frank and truthful manner. Presentation is critical because it strategically positions the change in the minds and hearts of those involved. As employees listen, their thoughts center on how they will fit into the planned change. Your presentation identifies the impact that each system and process change will have on the players on your team. Your focus is to help your employees to reframe their stories and to assess and appraise their capacity to work through the pending change.

You are then charged with devising steps for a smooth and chaos-free implementation of the organization's change initiative. You work with your employees to create a supportive environment. This allows them to work through what is about to happen, each in his or her unique way. While you keep the focus on the vision and benefits of the change, you also concentrate on the direct impact the change is having on your people. Unlike many managers, who fear interacting with employees during times of uncertainty and hide in their offices, you harness your courage. You open dialogue, hold conversations, and address all questions. This means being available and visible, walking around, and encouraging water cooler conversations.

While you encourage those employees who seem open and eager to new possibilities, you also become attentive to those employees who appear negative. They may be battling their own inner fears, wondering about new roles or if they will even have a job. Validate conflicting emotions and concerns, because these are very real to the people who hold them. Too often, managers just focus on the *how it is going to be* part of change and forget about the *what I am losing/giving up* part (Lewin 1951). Find the gaps and the dissonance. Be reassuring and help people adjust. Carefully assess what is working and what is not.

Skills for Leading Organizational Change

- Access avatar wisdom and leadership.
- Strategically position the change.
- Focus on employees; build new stories.
- Validate emotions and address fears.
- Open dialogue; be visible and available.
- Model the performance you desire.

Finally, be more conscious of your own behaviors and performance. Your employees are watching you! You may have your own fears and concerns about the planned change. Openly expressing these in positive ways can help others immensely. This shows your authenticity and that you are all together in the proverbial boat. Model the performance you want to see in others. Keep everything moving slowly forward, while adjustments are made around every facet of the change.

Steve, one of our coaching clients, successfully led the charge for change at ABC company. As vice president of operations, he was responsible for navigating this initiative, which affected numerous departments with varying levels of technology. Six months out from the "going live" date, Steve started meeting with his team of managers and assistants, outlining the dimensions of the change. This included projected timelines and exactly how each procedure affected the people involved. In his planning meetings, he engaged his managers in activities to help each one understand the impact that the changes would have on them and their people.

> *Things do not change, we change.*
> —Henry David Thoreau

Steve clearly defined the vision and outlined all the components of the intended goal. Discussions were encouraged about those aspects of the changes that employees might resist. Steve knew that his managers' ability to reduce the resistance to impending changes would be critical for the entire process to flow smoothly and be successful. He charged each member of his management team with formulating both process and people plans. The people plans included what actions would be needed to help team members make the right connections to the change.

The next few months were spent addressing all the issues. This meant going back to get closure on unresolved matters from the past. One issue was a downsizing that had occurred two years earlier. About 10 percent of the workforce had been released, and many employees had survivor's guilt. This was the 900-pound gorilla that still roamed the halls. Steve addressed it head-on. He specifically showed the differences in this change from what had happened during the downsizing. He created a "clean slate" for the new initiatives.

Early on in the change process, two things became apparent to Steve. One was the importance of communication. He worked hard creating the new picture of work and helped each person align his or her story with the reality of the forthcoming changes. There were posters adorning the halls that showed timelines of the process. Email and memos were used to update and inform everyone about what was happening every step of the way. Steve was visible and available. He projected the same positive attitude and encouragement to the daily ongoing operations and acknowledged frustrations when shifts occurred. Setbacks were shared as candidly and reliably as milestone successes.

The second element that aided Steve was the strong relationships he had already established. As employees asked questions about how their roles would change, he answered them honestly and openly. He held nothing back. And when he did not know the answer, he said so. Employees trusted him. That trust allowed for more risk taking. Mistakes that uncovered process problems were recognized as opportunities for solutions. There was lots of space for experimenting around the change process.

All our sources endorse the smooth transitions that happen when leadership is present and actively participating in any change process. Leaders use their vision to make the new initiatives attractive so that everyone believes in them and moves toward the change. Leaders also display the highest level of integrity when talking honestly and openly about issues that have an impact on people. More about the leader's role will be discussed in chapter 8. Until then, focus on building your own capacity to change and practice change on a regular basis.

Savvy Translation: Savvy managers know that organizations don't change; people change! They use vision to drive actions and create the right environment to inspire employees with new possibilities. They connect to their change avatar wisdom and carefully work with individual employees during times of uncertainty.

The Bottom Line: Embracing Change

Change is unsettling to the extent that you do not know what is going to happen and the impact it will have on you. You are charged to self-manage through change. From your role as manager, model behaviors and attitudes that create an environment that fosters change. Frame change into a coherent context around embedded beliefs and norms that inform actions. Validate the emotions and feelings that accompany the uncertainty of change. Support and inspire employees toward new actions during change. Successfully mastering any change presents a paradox. This means that you couple the benefits of sustainable change with the ability to shift gears the moment it becomes clear that another change is required. All your savvy skills and competencies work together to make the next change a logical move, strategically and smoothly executed.

We further extend your coaching with respect to two concepts, sacred cows and conscious choice. Sacred cows, those processes and beliefs that are held as ironclad, must be identified and challenged. These sacred cows exist both within your organization and in your personal and professional lives. They are the items that, when challenged, will generate the response *It's just the way we do things around here* or *That's just how I am!*

There can be no sacred cows where sustainable change lives. All processes and beliefs must be subject to scrutiny.

Consciously embracing change is a choice you make. As a manager, this sometimes means juggling two opposing balls. As you are charged to champion any organizational change initiative, you may realize that the proposed change will no longer mesh with how you want to work and what you want to do. Perhaps the new initiative is positioning your company to grow in a direction that differs from your own career goals and plans. At this point, you discern viable options. You choose to rethink and adjust your career goals, or you take the necessary steps to leave the company. You help foster the change, even as you negotiate your own smooth transition with honor and integrity. Knowing when to choose which action is all part of your personal, professional evolution in the process of embracing change.

Use It or Lose It

Write down the one key idea that you "got" as a takeaway from your reading. Then write down what you plan to do starting tomorrow to integrate this idea, practice it, and make it a habit.

1. What I got. _____

    _____

2. How I will use it tomorrow. _____

    _____

3. Which savvy skill(s) I am developing. _____

    _____

Reflection Interval

The process of change demands that you replace your old story with a new one. As you read the poem below, consider how often you hold on to habits and stay in your comfort zone. What does it take to get you to finally let go and embrace the new way?

An Autobiography in Five Chapters

By Portia Nelson—copyright 1993; reprinted with permission from her book
***There's a Hole in My Sidewalk* (Beyond Words Publishing)**

Chapter 1
I walk down the street.
There is a deep hole in the sidewalk.
I fall in.
I am lost. . . . I am hopeless.

It isn't my fault.
It takes forever to find a way out.

Chapter 2
I walk down the same street.
There is a deep hole in the sidewalk.
I pretend I don't see it.
I fall in again.
I can't believe I'm in the same place.
But it isn't my fault.
It still takes a long time to get out.

Chapter 3
I walk down the same street.
There is a deep hole in the sidewalk.
I see it is there.
I still fall in.... It's a habit.
My eyes are open.
I know where I am.
It is my fault.
I get out immediately.

Chapter 4
I walk down the same street.
There is a deep hole in the sidewalk.
I walk around it.

Chapter 5
I walk down a different street.

Coaching for Action: Driving Optimal Performance
Navigating the Steps of Change

Choose one situation that requires you to change. Focus on each of the steps in the Model for Consciously Embracing Change (table 4-1). On a piece of paper, write down each change element and then the aspect of the situation that relates to you. Identify the barriers you are encountering around each step. What new learning appears before your eyes? What new actions must you begin to take?

Practicing Change

One of the ways to become a change avatar is to practice change on a routine basis. Getting yourself comfortable with new things embeds new thoughts and emotions around new behaviors. Here are simple suggestions for you to try:

- Take a different route to work in the morning or home in the evenings.
- Sleep on the other side of the bed.
- Try new ethnic foods.
- Eat dessert first—at least once!
- Learn a new language.
- See a foreign film with English subtitles.
- Walk up the stairs instead of taking the elevator.
- Park in a different place at work or next time you visit the mall.
- Use a different color ink/paper for your next memo.
- Go for a walk on your lunch hour.

Embracing Change

A force field analysis is an important managerial tool. This instrument allows you to more clearly understand the various forces that can impact your decisions. Worksheet 4-1 is an adaptation of a worksheet developed by Kurt Lewin (1951). His premise was that you needed to focus on reducing the resistance to change even as you promote how "great" it will be once any change is implemented.

1. Choose a situation or problem you are currently experiencing at work or in your personal life.
2. Identify the forces that are driving your actions forward.
3. Identify the forces that are holding you back, that are preventing you from making a decision. These are often embedded in your fears and what you perceive as bringing you pain.
4. Now weigh each force with respect to its "hold" or power on you and your ability to accept any change. A force of 5 is very powerful and controlling, while a force of 1 is minor.
5. Choose one of your restraining forces and identify the specific actions and behaviors that you would need to take to reduce its power or hold over the situation and over you. How will you measure progress? What will be the visible signs that your resistance is diminishing? What will others be able to see?

Worksheet 4-1. Embracing Change

Problem or opportunity	Clearly state the problem that exists or the opportunity that you see.
Solution idea	Offer your solution or idea.
Pro forces	State the specific reasons you believe your solution or idea offers to solve the problem or capitalize on the opportunity. For each pro force, rate its intensity to drive the change (1 = low; 5 = high). 1. 2. 3. 4.
Con forces	Make the resistors real! Think of the reasons why employees will fear the change initiative you are suggesting. For each con force, rate its intensity to inhibit power or resistance to the change (1 = low; 5 = high). 1. 2. 3. 4.
Work through resistors	Lewin believed that reducing the resistance to change was a powerful process. Choose one resistor or con force to work on at a time. Answer the following questions as a means to develop a plan to reduce its impact. Resistor focus: _____ Specifically, what performance element must be different to accomplish the change? What resistor behaviors are embedded in the performance above that have to change? What will you do to reduce these resistors? What will you measure to show progress and results?

Lagniappe

Change can have a great impact on your focus and decision making. A map is a great tool to use to clarify your goals and vision and keep you moving forward. Make another visit to our authors' page at www.astd.org/SavvyManager. Download Lagniappe 3, the "Strategic Enterprise Map" worksheet, and begin to navigate your own successful path through change.

Demystifying Motivation

The kind of life you live tomorrow
begins in your mind today.

—Joe Batten

Build your savvy as you learn to

- enhance your knowledge of the fundamentals of motivation
- develop strategies to motivate yourself
- discern the role of rewards in motivating employees
- create a motivating workplace environment

What makes you strive to be the best at something? What is it that propels you to do more, to take that next step when it would be easier to just quit? There are forces in your life that compel you to continue to take action. One of these forces, and the focus of this chapter, is motivation. This critical competency, linked to your emotional intelligence, connects to the limbic part of the brain, the center that regulates feelings, impulses, and drives. Motivation is a topic that has been studied extensively and from many different perspectives. Both *content* and *process* theories have attempted to explain the what and how of motivation.

■ ■ ■

Real Time: Scott's Story

Things have been really difficult for all of us lately. Although our office is doing OK, sales are down companywide for the fifth straight quarter. Corporate is making changes left and right. Everyone is bracing for another round of early retirement offers, and the fear of layoffs is permeating the mood around here. My staff is overwhelmed and I'm not far behind them. Heck, it took me five minutes to psych myself up yesterday before I could even get out of my car to come into the building!

I'm worried about my staff. The energy in the department is just not there. George may be close to retirement age, but he isn't in a financial position to retire, even with a solid package. I see fear and anxiety in his eyes every time I go into his office to talk with him. The marketing people keep arguing about different strategies to increase sales. Allison continues to suggest new ideas, and Terry just keeps shooting them down. Christy, the new sales-person, seems to have moved beyond frustration. She was so excited six weeks ago when she first got here. I am not really sure what the source of her frustration is, but I'll put my money on the unrest she's witnessing all around her. She may even be tainted by those "old dogs" in sales. I hope she isn't out looking for another job already. To make matters worse, corpo-rate has frozen all salary increases until further notice. What do I say to the people with yearly reviews coming up?

At our morning briefings, I keep telling my staff to just stay the course and that now is the time for everyone to go the extra mile. They just look at me, nodding their heads. They're doing their jobs but not extending themselves above and beyond minimum efforts. We clearly have serious morale issues here. This is the stuff they didn't teach me in management classes!

Although I can't change what corporate is doing, what I can and need to do really fast is change the energy around here. I just need to create that first spark. I'm struggling about how to do it in a credible way. How do I create a motivating environment for people who are working in fear? What can I do to keep my own motivation high?

■ ■ ■

Motivation is defined as internal energy. It is a mental process that moves a person toward action. Connecting to this energy source is the catalyst that stimulates you to achieve your specific objectives. Motivation is unique for every person and every sit-uation. What is common among all are its effects. Motivation soars when you like what you are doing. It breeds confidence and increases optimism. It provides you with the perseverance to stay focused on your goals. It also allows you to rebound more easily when your plans hit that proverbial bump in the road.

Clearly, motivation is an essential ingredient for career success. It is highly desirable as an employee characteristic and a genuine consideration when managing. And finding that unique approach, the right "chemistry" for each person, is part of the challenge for you as a manager. Your role in managing both yourself and your team is to connect the theoretical abstraction of this energy, called motivation, into action strategies that produce results.

Motivation is one of those realities that operates under the radar. Its value and importance as both a personal competency and managerial tool require us to bring it front and center as part of your savvy development. Our coaching for you in this chapter focuses on two critical aspects of motivation. First, we want to enhance your current knowledge and understanding about motivation energy. The fundamentals of motivation include motivational direction, extrinsic and intrinsic control mechanisms, and the significant role that attitude plays in motivation. You will find facts and alternative perspectives on several of the myths about motivation. Once you understand how motivation works, you can integrate some of the suggested strategies to better motivate yourself and to create a motivating environment for others. Several underlying questions should help guide your coaching on motivation:

- What energizes your actions?
- What captures your attention to get you moving?
- What is it that keeps you going to reach your goal?
- What stops you?

Debunking the Myths

Motivation denotes many things to many people. Gaining clarity around what is true about motivation and what is "an old wives' tale" will empower you and your employees to stay motivated. As you consider table 5-1, which distinguishes the myths from the facts, relate them to your own personal experiences. Challenge your perspectives. Use the table's savvy translations to modify your thinking and develop more effective strategies for motivating yourself and your team.

> *The difference between a successful person and others is not a lack of strength, not a lack of knowledge, but rather in a lack of will.*
>
> —Vincent T. Lombardi

Table 5-1. Myths and Facts about Motivation

Myth	Fact	Savvy Translation
I can motivate other people!	Motivation is an internal force, an "inside" job. Managers can stimulate, inspire, model, and influence. But they can also manipulate. The real energy of motivation emanates uniquely from within each individual.	Savvy managers create a motivational space, an environment within which employees find and connect to their motivation. They look for ways, through their words and actions, to serve as a role model of motivation for the members of their team.
Money is the best motivator!	Money is a finite resource and is insufficient as a long-term motivator. Money serves more to keep people from being dissatisfied, than to actually motivate performance.	Savvy managers recognize how the economic utility of work fits into the motivation equation. They know the difference between manipulation (which can become rather costly over the long haul) and motivation. Money is used judiciously for any motivational value.
Fear is a good motivator!	Fear only motivates in the short term; as a means to get *away from* the threat or minimize the concern. Fear, threats, and punishment are seldom sustainable and certainly not a recommended management practice.	Savvy managers know that threats and intimidation do not spark natural motivators in a person who strives for excellence. Rather, they utilize strategies that build confidence, encourage risk taking, inspire, and empower performance.
Everyone is motivated in the same way, by the same thing.	Motivation is unique to each person. Looking deeper lets you connect to each person's true desires. This fires up his or her motivation and inspires his or her actions.	Savvy managers pay attention and listen to their employees. They know that the easiest way to discover what really motivates employees is to just ask. They find ways to help employees utilize their personal motivators at work.
People are paid to work and do a job. Efforts to motivate are a waste of time.	All efforts to help maximize performance and ensure results are not only worth your efforts but are a large part of your accountability as a manager. Companies need more than employees who just show up for a paycheck.	Savvy managers know that by simply applying sound principles of leadership, communication, and learning, they tap into those internal resources that allow their employees to find purpose and grow their emotional intelligence around motivation. They actively seek to hire motivated people and create a culture where it flourishes.

Source: Adapted from McNamara (1999).

Directional Power: Pain versus Pleasure

Motivation requires your attention. We know from research that there are two critical aspects of motivation that control us. The first is pleasure or satisfaction, that which brings you a sense of meaning, purpose, and fulfillment. At the other end of the motivation continuum is pain or fear, those situations and events that you perceive as threats. You may be pursuing pleasure (however or whatever you perceive pleasure to be), which is designated as *toward* motivation. Or, you are avoiding pain (again, however or whatever you perceive that to be), which is referred to as *away from* motivation. The challenge becomes one of recognizing exactly what is motivating you at a particular moment. When you compare that to what you claim to want, you can then act consciously toward that end (Dyer 1992).

It is in this dichotomy that you witness the challenge presented as motivation. At a biological, physical, and psychological level, we all have developed both aspects of motivational input. You can be motivated to move *toward* a situation: taking actions that drive you toward joy, fulfillment, comfort, and happiness. You can be equally motivated to move away from things that you think are painful or will bring you stress, fear, or distress. There are dangerous places, unsafe actions, poor choices, and negative thinking that merit moving *away from*. Each direction offers a very different way of being motivated, and both are highly useful in different situations (Andreas and Faulkner 1994).

Although we all use both directions to some degree, we usually favor one direction more than the other. Take the example of your morning routine. You might be rushing off to work in the morning worried about what being late would cause: another speeding ticket, clients waiting, your boss shouting, dirty looks from co-workers. This is *away from* motivation because your motivation to get to work on time is initiated by consequences you want to avoid. You get up when the alarm goes off to avoid the negative consequence you associate with being late.

> *The greatest discovery of my generation is that a human being can alter his life by altering his attitudes of mind.*
>
> —William James

If you are a manager who relies on *away from* motivation, you focus on punishment and threats to get your employees to work a certain way. And, although this may seem necessary to produce results from some of your people in the short term, long-term results are never sustainable. And the results that you do produce are never as good as the results you might realize through conscious, positive motivated intentions. Threats and punishment do not bring out the best in people. Savvy managers know that fear is not a reliable or recommended tactic for motivating anyone!

To better understand *toward* motivation, visualize an exciting project at work. Note your energy level. You are enthusiastic, inspired by the challenge, and eager to get to work. You even lose track of the time while focusing on the project. This is *toward*

> *I never did a day's work in my life.*
> *It was all fun.*
>
> —Thomas Edison

motivation. Accomplishing something that you want becomes your driving force. It keeps you energized and leads you through each next step.

Consider how Harry and Darla are utilizing different motivational directions. Far from being negative, Harry is applying *away from* motivation when he voices concerns regarding problems and the obstacles he sees with the current project. Because Darla isn't seeing the problems that are so huge to Harry, her readiness to take action on her part of the project (*toward* motivation) shows up as rashness or shortsightedness to Harry. Darla and Harry are each motivated in their own, unique way. Both perspectives are needed to make the project a success. Once Harry and Darla come to terms with each other's modes of operating and motivational needs, these differences will diminish and they will work together effectively.

There is no right or wrong to either direction. People are equally successful when attached to either *toward* or *away from* motivation as a way of life. What is obvious from the study of motivation direction is that the *toward* orientation is more goal directed, and the *away from* orientation is more focused on identifying and solving problems. As the manager, you need to recognize and acknowledge the interplay of motivational direction as it occurs. Your role in such discussions is to keep everyone focused on results and minimize group conflicts by acknowledging all perspectives. Recognize motivational direction and harness the energy from both styles when they emerge in group dynamics.

 Savvy Translation: Savvy managers know that motivation happens uniquely for every person. They validate the concerns of those using *away from* motivation and empower those driven by *toward* motivation. They know that both are effective approaches.

Pushing the Right Buttons

When Sara was applying for a part-time sales position, the manager asked her if she was motivated by money. She replied honestly that it was not her primary motivation. She was more inspired by a strong sense of helping customers and educating them to make the best purchase for their needs. Money, however, was a prime motivator for the manager doing the hiring. Making his sales numbers, not creating relationships, was his focus during transactions with customers. Neither was wrong. The differences carried potential conflict between the manager, who focused on closing a sale, and Sara, whose focus was service, regardless of whether an actual sale occurred. Do you think Sara got that job?

The example above opens the discussion to an important distinction: the source and power of the control mechanisms that affect your motivation. These mechanisms show up as rewards or consequences. Whenever the reward mechanism is separate, or outside the person doing the work (your boss, co-worker, your family or fans), it is considered *extrinsic*. Extrinsic rewards include such things as salaries, raises, bonuses, accolades, notoriety, and other tangible goods. Remember the line "Show me the money!" made famous in the movie *Jerry McGuire*? Extrinsic rewards can hold great power over you. When their appeal is strong, you can more easily be manipulated. The use of extrinsic rewards as a strategy should never be confused with real motivation.

Naturally satisfying rewards that you control are called *intrinsic*. The reward emanates from within you, derived from your inner sense of contribution and your feelings of accomplishment. You know that feeling! It's the satisfaction that shows up when you really stretch to reach your goal. Or that internal glow from the random acts of kindness you do for family or co-workers, just because. Intrinsic rewards abound when you know you have done your best, regardless of what anyone else knows or says to you. Intrinsic reward, that true motivation from your core, is always about your sense of personal satisfaction.

Intrinsic rewards are supported by your savvy skills of self-managing, reflecting, and acting consciously. It is one of the reasons why we coach clients to find work about which they are passionate. Loving your work is one sure way to realize intrinsic motivation! When you experience success from serving customers or from creating products, you feel valued

> *The right people will do the right things and deliver the best results they're capable of, regardless of the incentive system.*
>
> —Jim Collins

and highly motivated to do it again and again. The more you achieve a sense of personal value and expand your feelings of self-worth from your efforts, the greater the motivation to continue performing that work. Internal levels of satisfaction make you feel empowered and self-assured. Because it is intrinsic, it is the highest form of reward: iterative, continual, and self-sustaining.

Authentic motivation moves people to performance levels that manipulative tactics never come close to realizing. Think about your own management experience. Have

> *Keep your mind on the things*
> *you want and off the things*
> *you don't want.*
>
> —Earl Nightingale

you ever been in a situation where you treated two of your employees the exact same way? One was motivated and produced great work; the other was not. With the same rewards being placed before each, only one performed. It supports the underlying principle that motivation is truly a unique experience and that one person cannot really motivate another person.

Achieving a deeper understanding of both intrinsic and extrinsic rewards is the first step in your strategy to create an environment where the behavior of your employees will be influenced or driven to action—naturally. Working collaboratively with your employees, tap into their natural interests and talents. Set the context and offer the opportunity for your team to act consciously. When employees pursue goals that interest them, the rewards realized are of considerable valuable, in and of themselves. In the right environment, everyone achieves success on both personal and company-wide levels.

In the final analysis, it should be clear that you can (perhaps) manipulate someone to do something with the promise of extrinsic reward, but that motivation, as an inside job, holds more power. You need to remember that only you can motivate yourself. Take time to reflect about your own reward mechanisms. Do intrinsic rewards create the same action responses as extrinsic rewards? Which reward mechanism is more powerful for you?

 Savvy Translation: Savvy managers know the difference between motivation and manipulation. They choose authentic motivation and artfully work to tune in to each person's intrinsic reward system.

Attitude Is Everything!

Your attitude permeates every aspect of your life and has a tremendous impact on your motivation, your performance, and ultimately your success. Attitude—defined as a mental state, a disposition, an opinion, or a feeling—is like motivation in that it is an inside job. This powerful component of your emotional domain connects with your feelings and mood. It originates from your thoughts and directs your actions. Woody Allen was quoted as saying "Ninety percent of life is about just showing up," and the addition of the phrase "with a positive attitude" makes his comment relevant and applicable to this discussion. Realize, now, that attitude is absolutely a matter of choice—your choice.

Attitude develops as a transparent sequence within the domains of language, emotion, and body. In any situation or event, your feelings intertwine with your rational thoughts. From this process, you create a story about yourself and the relationship to this event and the people who are involved. Yes, it is the

> *Ability is what you're capable of doing. Motivation determines what you do. Attitude determines how well you do it.*
>
> —Lou Holtz

same "story" we discussed in chapter 4. This story embeds itself in your mind and shows up outwardly in how you express yourself verbally and present yourself physically. Your attitude, then, is presumed and labeled by others based on what you say and how you act. For better or worse, your attitude affects the attitudes of your team, work groups, and whole organization. Your motivation shows up as performance that is directly linked to your attitude.

The Choice Is Yours

Opting to have a positive attitude is a matter of applying your savvy skill of acting consciously and choosing to see events through a positive prism. We liken this to what Wayne Dyer (2004) labels the power of intention. You develop this ability through learning and the practice of reprogramming your thinking. Your savvy skill of self-managing plays a tremendously important role here. You change your actions to align with your new affirming thoughts. You keep your conscious mind focused on the positive side, seeing people as intentionally wanting the best for everyone. You consciously choose to find the good rather than fixating on the negative. When you observe yourself sliding down the negative path, you self-manage. You stop and self-correct.

Looking for the good things from situations and reframing negative events as learning experiences takes practice and the intentional goal of maintaining a positive mindset. Two highly effective tools can help you find and maintain your positive attitude. These include affirmations, statements asserting something you really desire to be true for yourself, and visualization, the ability to form clear pictures. Consider these two examples. Kathy, wanting to shift her somewhat negative outlook on life to one that was more positive, chose to practice an affirmation. Her affirmation was "I am healthy, . . . I am happy, . . . I am in control, . . . I am terrific!" At first, her practice of reciting this daily seemed awkward and phony. However, she was amazed at how soon this conscious practice became routine and, even more so, how quickly it manifested as a reality in her life. Her new thoughts truly guided how she was showing up and the decisions she was making.

Ken used visualization to help him move from a losing sales streak in which he seemed stuck. He began to picture himself dressed like a successful salesman, connecting with the client in his office during his presentation, and feeling confident and poised in closing the sale. Practicing this visualization in his car while driving to appointments moved him from sporadic sales success to having one of the highest closure rates in his company. His shift in attitude made all the difference for Ken.

Both visualization and affirmations are tools that you can use personally and when managing. Keep your company vision alive and in front of your team on a regular basis. Revise it if what you have is not meaningful for you and the staff. Create affirmations that support your positive attitude and give direction and flow to your efforts. Share language and create affirmations that keep your energy high and positive. Think of Nike and its successful, simple phrase "Just do it."

> *The thing always happens that you really believe in; and the belief in a thing makes it happen.*
> —Frank Lloyd Wright

Although you can't change a person's attitude, as a savvy manager you can choose to take particular conscious actions. Always remember the often-used adage "Hire for attitude, train for skills!" Really pay attention to the attitudes that show up in your workplace, especially during challenging times. Attitude is contagious; misery loves company! Negative attitudes spread faster than any positive attitude ever could. Quickly addressing an employee's shift to negative behavior will yield the greatest results for both that person and your team. You can offer critical, constructive support, and perhaps some additional resources or insights from your own experiences. As you coach your employees, look for ways that move them forward into choosing a positive attitude over any negative perspective.

 Savvy Translation: Savvy managers are vigilant about attitude. They are keenly sensitive to the prevailing attitude and confront employees quickly and decisively when a perceived negative attitude reveals itself.

Strategically Managing Motivation

If we accept that motivation is an inside job, then the question becomes clear: *What will you do to help your employees motivate themselves to greater levels of performance?* Please recognize that the language here is critical. As a manager, you will not really motivate your staff. You will inspire, influence, stimulate, support, encourage, and challenge them.

Motivation has a peculiar twist. Although you cannot really motivate another person, it is possible to demotivate them. Although this doesn't seem to be an equitable proposition, it is yet another challenge facing you as a manager.

> *Take charge of your attitude. Don't let someone else choose it for you.*
> —H. Jackson Brown

You can use various strategies to create a place where people find their motivation—where you remove the elements that could demotivate. Managing with the goal of helping employees stay motivated is an ongoing process, not a single task. These strategies will sound familiar because they are part of being an artful leader, an inspiring change avatar, and a truly effective communicator. They offer solutions to help you create the results you want.

- *Identify your own motivators.* Knowing what motivates you is the very first step to staying motivated. Once you discover your own motivators, approach your staff and help them discover theirs. Configure your job (and the jobs of your employees) to allow for everyone's natural motivators to work.
- *Make rewards positive and personal.* Help employees meet their own goals in ways that both challenge and reward them. Effectively tap their natural motivation by giving immediate and appropriate positive reinforcement as close to the event deserving the merit as possible. Deliver your feedback with sincerity and truth.
- *Eliminate threats and punishments.* Stress and pressure keep the focus on fears, not on performance or goals. Threatening is counter to your creation of an environment of cooperation and openness. Note that removing punishments does not mean that there are no consequences! All actions have consequences, which are distinctly different from punishments.
- *Make acting consciously part of your culture.* Wherever appropriate, allow your employees flexibility and choices concerning the tasks for which they are directly accountable. Compliance rules when there is never a choice. Giving the responsibility of choice supports both commitment to extraordinary outcomes and professional development.
- *Align personal goals with company goals.* Create motivated partners by showing employees the big picture. Explain how their tasks vitally contribute to success for the whole organization.
- *Practice focused listening.* The motivating power of attentive listening validates your employees and enhances respect and trust. Listening and

staying connected with them unlock their potential and sustain their performance.

- *Be a role model.* Demonstrate your own motivation. Be animated, realistic, enthusiastic, and focused. Set the pace and create the right environment. Your employees are watching you; they will likely emulate what you model. Nothing deflates motivation in an employee more quickly than a manager who preaches one thing but practices another!

- *Pay attention to your employees.* The acronyms WIIFM—*What's in it for me?*—and PMMFI—*Please make me feel important!*—offer two good starting points. Interact with your employees while remaining consciously focused on meeting their needs and making them feel important. Make it a routine to get out of your office and onto the work floor. Let your employees get to know you. Strong relationships are great motivators!

The Bottom Line: Demystifying Motivation

Your true motivation emerges from the emotional domain. As you have seen, motivation includes competencies like your intrinsic drive toward achievement, an ability to commit to accomplishing set goals, your own initiative, and the readiness to seek out and act on opportunities. It relies on developing optimism that allows you to move through obstacles and to overcome problems. Motivation and attitude work in harmony. Your tenacity and resiliency are also critical attributes. These help you remain focused on your set course.

We all desire to gain something for our efforts. Stuff matters! The problem arises when material rewards and external validation for work are overused and when the inner reward that we gain from the work itself is never fully realized or appreciated. This is at the heart of motivation. You need to realize which rewards are most meaningful to you and their origination point. Does your own internal reward mechanism live as a strong motivator? Reflecting on the source of your own motivational triggers is one part of the motivation dynamic.

Finally, we want to coach you through the greatest challenge: creating a motivating workplace, where people feel safe and where trust is the foundation of all interactions. As a savvy manager, you actively look for every opportunity to inspire and direct all employees' energies toward effective and meaningful work. You model this positive capability. And because your employees are watching you, you make the conscious choice to get up, get out of your office, and interact with your team every day regardless of how busy you are with your own projects. The gut check about creating this motivational space lies in your own self-awareness and in your answers to the following coaching questions—which are sure to ignite a lively discussion with your team. You only need to have the courage to ask these questions of both yourself and your employees. Then be quiet, listen, and reflect.

Coaching questions to ponder:

- What is it that motivates me (you) to perform?
- What inspires me (you) to give a job my (your) best efforts?
- What do I (you) want to realize from the work I (you) do?
- What type of environment do I (you) need to perform at my (your) best?
- What management style is most motivating for me (you)?
- How do my (your) actions align with my (your) values?
- What actions might I (you) be taking that are no longer serving me (you)?
- What types of reinforcement/rewards do I (you) need?
- What role does reinforcement from others play for me (you)?

Use It or Lose It

Write down the one key idea that you "got" as a takeaway from your reading. Then write down what you plan to do starting tomorrow to integrate this idea, practice it, and make it a habit.

1. What I got. _____

   _____

2. How I will use it tomorrow. _____

   _____

3. Which savvy skill(s) I am developing. _____

   _____

Reflection Interval

This story should expand your thinking about motivation. After you are finished reading about the frogs, consider the times when you might have been stuck like the frog in the story. Think about the internal and external forces you use to help yourself get or stay motivated, and the people who act as ongoing sources of motivation in your life.

Frogs in the Pit

By Roy D. Follendore III—copyright 2000
(http://noisetoknowledge.com/frogs.htm); used with permission

*Sometimes even the best-intentioned friends
can become your worst enemy.*

A long time before man knew how to speak, a band of frogs were traveling through the woods, croaking for females that lived in a nearby pond, when two of them fell into a deep pit. All the other frogs gathered around the pit. When they looked over the edge and saw how deep the pit was, they told the unfortunate frogs they would never get out. The two frogs ignored all the comments and tried to jump up and out of the pit.

The other frogs kept screaming at them to stop, because they were as good as dead. Finally, one of the frogs took heed to what the other frogs were saying and simply gave up. He fell down and simply died peacefully.

But the other frog continued to jump as hard as he could. Once again, the crowd of frogs yelled at him to stop the pain and suffering and just relax and die. At this instead, he jumped even harder. . . and finally made it out.

When he got out, the other frogs shouted at him, "Why did you continue jumping? We were your friends looking out for your interest. Didn't you hear us? We were trying to help you!"

At first the frog could not tell why they looked so upset. The frog then patiently explained to them that he was hard of hearing, almost deaf.

"You were my friends, and for that reason I thought you were encouraging me to survive so that I might find the pond!" said the surviving frog, hopping on his way, leaving the others to their fate. He went on that day to find all the females in their pond, who were delighted to share their genes with such a strong example of an amphibian, even if he could not hear too well.

Coaching for Action: Driving Optimal Performance
More/Less/Start/Stop!

1. Recognizing what truly motivates you is important. Ask yourself this question: Is there anything I am doing right now, knowing what I now know, that I wouldn't do if I were starting over today? Make a list of these items and then tackle them one at a time with the goal of changing your behavior.
2. To achieve the goals in your life, ask yourself these questions (write down your answers and act on your findings):
   a. What do I need to do more of?
   b. What do I need to do less of?
   c. What do I need to start doing?
   d. What do I need to stop doing?

The Four Reallys

This exercise comes from Wayne Dyer, an expert in the field of motivation and one of our admired gurus. On a sheet of paper, write down your responses to each question.

Answer the questions slowly, one at a time, perhaps over a span of four days (one iteration of the question each day) to allow time to reflect on your responses. Do not rush the process:

1. What is it that I really want?
2. What is it that I really, really want?
3. What is it that I really, really, really want?
4. What is it that I really, really, really, really want?

Lagniappe

Motivation plays such an important role in everyone's life. Visit the Learning Annex 3 at www.astd.org/SavvyManager to refresh your learning about the content and process theories of motivation. Study the sources of motivation to identify where your motivation takes root. And then help your employees locate the source of their motivational energy.

Mastering Communication

The danger in communication is the illusion
that it has been accomplished.

—George Bernard Shaw

Build your savvy as you learn to

- define effective communication
- generate meaningful conversations through dialogue
- utilize different conversation types to achieve desired results
- choose speech acts to effectively accomplish communication

Managing in complex times demands competent and effective communications throughout your organization. Shouting orders and directions to employees has evolved into more fluid and open conversations involving people at all levels of the company. Credible data tells us that full involvement consistently leads to better results. Generating effective conversations creates ownership of results, builds commitment from all employees, and is naturally motivating. Conversations are the lifeblood of communication and are the focus of your coaching in this chapter. We want you to become a powerful conversationalist.

■ ■ ■

Real Time: Colleen's Story

I'm sorry. I just don't get it. How hard is it to hit the "reply" key and let someone know that you received a document? Pick up the phone and leave a message that the fax arrived! Tell a person when you're sending something important that requires feedback! In our high-tech world, we really need to make a more conscious effort to close the communication loop. It's out of control!

It's Wednesday. Friday is the presentation for a major client, and none of my people are working together. Two weeks ago Brady, the project manager, sent an email. No one bothered to respond as to whether they got it, so he assumed they did! A week went by before he found out that Carol in accounting never got the email. She came up with great figures using the wrong data! The really crazy thing is that they are just across the hall from each other! How much sense does that make? So now we have 48 hours to scramble before the presentation.

As if that weren't enough, Becky just told me that she has not received authorization for the new hardware I ordered for Friday's demonstration. And she is refusing to process the order without Jacob's approval. Even with my assurances that it's approved, she won't budge. I've left urgent messages for Jacob on his cellphone and by email and haven't heard anything back from him yet. It's like the big black hole of silence!

When did we forget how to communicate? We've become so caught up in the technology we've forgotten how to just talk to each other. I can't remember the last time I had a clear, articulate conversation with someone! These snafus are driving all of us crazy. We've got to get a grip on how to work together more effectively; just learning how to better communicate with each other would be a great start. As director, I am ultimately accountable. Where do I begin? How do I get people to listen to one another? We need to get better at sharing ideas and using communication tools that work for us, not against us.

■ ■ ■

Communication can be defined simply as a process of transforming thoughts and ideas into messages transferred between senders and receivers. Communication occurs through any number of mediums—like reading, talking, listening, and writing. The process includes all the components of language (word choices, tone, pitch, meanings), as well as the more subtle aspects of nonverbal signals. Research studies suggest that your verbal message, the actual words you speak, reflects only about 7 to 10 percent of your message. The greatest impact of your communication comes from your body language (55 to 58 percent) and your vocal tone (38 to 40 percent), including the pitch, volume, and rhythm of your speech.

When you examine all these components, the inherent complexity of communication shines through. Although most people think of communication as a language act, communication actually takes place within all three of the domains: language, emotion, and body. It is about what actually happens around a message and how the participants establish the space in which the conversation materializes. It requires all your savvy skills operating together to do it well. A vital part of your coaching is to realize how both the emotional and the physical domains affect your daily conversations and, thus, bear upon your outcomes.

Using the art of conversation as our platform, the goal of this chapter is to help you develop your communication competencies. Our unique approach to this topic is anything but traditional. We address three aspects of the communication process that are instrumental in developing your managerial expertise: specific types of conversations, focused listening, and speech acts. Each is presented with a savvy application to enhance your communication prowess. Dialogue is introduced as a flow and exchange in conversation that moves communication to its highest level.

The Nuts and Bolts

Two very broad goals should be at the core of all of your communication activities. Your first goal is to be understood: to have your message received and comprehended, just as you intended. Being understood includes the challenge of transforming your ideas and thoughts into words that have shared value and common meaning between yourself and another. You may know exactly what

> *I know that you believe you understand what you think I said, but I am not sure you realize that what you heard is not what I meant.*
>
> —attributed to Robert McCloskey

you are *thinking* and trying to express, but having that happen is not always the case. Meanings do not come prepackaged in human communication.

Your second goal is to have actions or results occur that are aligned with what you communicated and your desired intentions. Consider exactly how this works for you as a manager. You spend part of the time at your weekly staff meeting communicating expectations to your team. When your team responds by acknowledging the goals and objectives you have communicated, you know you have been understood. That's good, but insufficient. What you want is for your communication to produce the desired results. When your team takes action, performing as you expected, then you have met your second goal. You have been effective in the communication process (King 1979).

> *Everything you say and do,*
> *as well as everything you fail to say,*
> *will communicate a message. You*
> *cannot not influence people!*
>
> —Jack Mackey

Unfortunately, communication sometimes misses the mark. Think about Ted, for example. Recently, he started hearing complaints that his employees were dissatisfied about the information they were receiving regarding operations. He interpreted this to mean that his employees wanted to know more. He rushed to produce a company newsletter, fully expecting this written communication to fix the problem. He never asked questions or discussed the complaints, nor did he engage in conversations with anyone on his team. As you might expect, Ted completely missed the message his employees were sending. They did not really want *more* information; they were confused and concerned about what they were already hearing. They thought management was making changes without their input or concern for their welfare. They felt excluded. They had ideas about their work processes that they wanted to share. Ted's actions, while well intended, did not produce the desired results.

When responses like Ted's are not aligned with sent messages, a communication breakdown has occurred. These breakdowns happen all the time for any number of reasons. They could be the result of an unforeseen problem, or simply that someone did not get your message. People might disagree with you, or choose to ignore your message. Your receiver may want to pursue a different alternative or be uncomfortable about how to speak with you about an opposing point of view. Many breakdowns occur when emotions get triggered. Something or someone "pushes your buttons." One common reaction is to disengage, shut down, and stop communicating. The other is to overreact, get loud, possibly abusive, and try to make your points regardless of how they may be received. In both reactions, effective exchange is lost.

Meaningful conversations are the pulse of effective communication. You must learn how to *be* with the communication. This means that you listen openly and empathically. You reflect and become very aware of *who* you are being when you are speaking and listening. You must be alert to potential breakdowns in communication by observing yourself and those engaged in conversations. Your ability to wisely choose appropriate conversational actions reflects your abilities to respond with heightened awareness to the challenges of being heard and understood.

 Savvy Translation: Savvy managers know they hold the keys to effective conversations. They listen with mind and heart to understand the full meaning behind the words. Their actions encourage honest, open exchanges and solidify relationships. They handle breakdowns with grace and decisive actions.

Conversations as Dialogue

Your ability to generate meaningful conversations is at the heart of your becoming a savvy manager. Simply explained, conversation is the act of talking together, collaboratively. Conversations set the tone, establish your culture, and give meaning to work in your organization. Within conversations, ideas, thoughts, and feelings are exchanged. People feel heard. From the give and take in a conversation, perceptions of a topic's important facets are heightened. Shared meanings develop, allowing new possibilities to emerge. Conversations engage people to come to solutions that are better than what any one person could reason alone. Relationships between all parties are strengthened from meaningful conversations.

> *Conversations are dances that literally find their own way, based upon the judgment and skill of the dancers.*
>
> —David A. Schmaltz

The flow or meaningful exchange of a conversation is called dialogue. In *The Fifth Discipline*, Peter Senge (1990) presents the work of Bohm and the concept of dialogue. Dialogue is the essence of conversation. It is a process of receiving what is said and reflecting on its various shades of meaning. Probing to evoke ideas and heighten understanding of the best possible choices or actions to take then follows. Sometimes, dialogue takes on the image of a tennis game, with the ball going fast and furiously over the net as ideas are exchanged. At other times, the conversation might resemble the game of badminton, where ideas and thoughts float gently from one player to another with each person building upon or enriching the previous comments.

Dialogue asks you to suspend your assumptions. What you think, believe, and want to do must be available for reconsideration and adjustment. Dialogue creates shared space. Dialogue conversations have a collective intention, a joint, creative activity. Although there clearly is a subject in dialogue, there is no preconceived outcome. When your mind is open to the interaction and the flow of dialogue, people involved in the conversation practice listening *with* one another. A more collaborative spirit lives within dialogue, guiding interactions and helping everyone gain clarity and insight. Through dialogue, you and your team produce your desired results, which would have been unlikely without the high level of collaboration that happens with such meaningful conversations (Wheatley 2002).

In dialogue, people engage in conversations as colleagues. This establishes a positive tone and supports collegial relationships that override rank or positions of power within your organization. When you accept that all contributions have merit, you empower everyone to contribute more freely. Everyone knows that his or her comments will be respected. There is mutually accepted shared responsibility for making the conversation flow. When it's your turn to talk, you talk. When it's your turn to listen, you listen. Trust and personal safety play a key role in successful dialogues.

> *A conversation is the natural process by which people live together, create together, and change together.*
> —Margaret Wheatley

During dialogue, the communication process shifts from one of defending a point of view to a process aimed at exchanging ideas and increasing levels of understanding. Without this critical shift, there is only talking *at* someone. Can you remember the times you may have argued vociferously for your point of view, closing yourself off to anything but your own opinion? You held your assumptions as the way it must be, as fact or truth. From this place, you might have pontificated, engaging in soliloquies or diatribes that dominated the conversation. You might have made personal attacks or "sniper" comments or have been loud and overbearing. Or maybe you talked just to hear yourself talk! We can confirm that this was not dialogue. It is reasonable and understandable that you have ideas and opinions. The distinction here is that in dialogue, your opinions don't have you!

The key coaching point of this discussion is that your conversational competence revolves around your ability to engage in dialogue. Through dialogue conversations, you are challenged to understand who you really are as an individual and as a player on the team. Savvy managers know how to self-manage, revealing their own perceptions and owning the expression of their ideas. They consciously probe and evoke in ways that invite discussion and true collaboration during conversations. These distinctions are the essence of meaningful and effective conversations that build relationships, drive actions, and produce results.

 Savvy Translation: Savvy managers practice strategies that set the mood for meaningful dialogue. They know that exceptional results are born in shared space where people give freely of their talents.

Types of Conversations

Not all conversations are created equal! When you appreciate both the openness and the flow that dialogue offers, you are ready to address the different possible conversations available. Julio Olallo (2000) directs you to notice that different types of conversations will direct you toward specific outcomes or actions and will reduce the risk of breakdowns. Knowing what type of conversation needs to take place enables you to prepare. It requires you to set clear expectations regarding desired outcomes for every conversation you hold. It also challenges you to be effective, thinking "on your feet" when you are drawn into a conversation you may be unprepared to have. It takes courage at that critical moment to request that the conversation be postponed. Savvy managers know that the best performance results happen in the workplace when everyone is poised and ready for the same type of conversation.

For example, consider Taylor, a department manager who often sends that nefarious "I need to talk to you!" email. Without giving any insight on the topic to be discussed, Taylor might be unaware of the impact of such a communication or could be on some kind of power trip. Any conversation about to occur with Taylor has already been compromised. It would have been just as easy, and significantly more productive, for this email to have contained something in the subject line or text regarding the matter to be discussed. This would have allowed the person meeting with Taylor time to prepare to participate as an effective equal in the conversation.

The strategy you need to develop is one of questioning yourself before you ever begin a conversation or use any communication medium. Again, the purpose is about intention and outcome. You need to pause and ask yourself these powerful questions: *What type of conversation will move me closer to my desired outcome? What must I do personally to enable an effective, unemotional, forward-moving conversation?* To coordinate actions to produce the desired results, you must learn to facilitate the right conversation at the right time.

Tables 6-1 through 6-3 identify three different types of conversations. Study the distinctions within each type. Our coaching here will help you to think differently and initiate new practices that generate more effective conversations in your workplace.

Speculative conversations (table 6-1) are focused on inquiry. You might frequently indulge in *self-talk* conversations that let you gain clarity about what you really want. This is a good practice to cultivate for finding direction before you ever talk with your team. The more important focus in speculative conversations occurs in group sessions, where you ask participants to consider possibilities, to "think outside the box." Speculative conversations, often called brainstorming, are usually held to generate a list of possible alternatives. That is always the outcome goal. These are conversations that happen in the first part of a strategy meeting where dialogue flows around options and possibilities. Realize the distinction being made here. Speculative conversations are not action conversations. Action conversations come later and require a different format, tone, and outcome goal.

For example, consider Kim, a project manager who has learned to effectively utilize different types of conversations. Kim believes in the power of generating as many ideas as possible for consideration. She takes great pride in making her speculative conversations fun events. She usually brings snacks and toys to energize the people present. She maintains control of her *imagination sessions* by strictly adhering to a one-hour time limit. After the meeting, she knows the creative juices will still be flowing. She then sets up a group intranet site and extends the invitation to continue the session online, marking a cutoff point for ending the imagination session.

Action conversations (table 6-2) set a direction that demands execution. Decisions and choices are made; implementation becomes the focus. Action conversations clearly describe the goal and identify roles in achieving it. Here communication centers on

Table 6-1. Speculative Conversations

Type of Conversation	Distinctions
Conversations about conversations	Set the frame regarding the subject matter of the conversation. Answer the question: What conversation do we need to have to accomplish what we claim to want?
Conversations for possible action	Offer a full range of possible actions to be explored to discern what will produce the desired outcomes. It is here that shared concerns emerge. This is often called brainstorming. Creative thinking and innovation are utilized here.

Source: Adapted from Newfield Network, Inc.

Table 6-2. Action Conversations

Type of Conversation	Distinctions
Conversations for action	When something needs to happen and action is required, a full range of requests, offers, and commitments is made to achieve the mutually desired outcomes. Conditions for satisfaction and assessment standards are clarified.
Conversations about breakdowns	These conversations acknowledge that a problem has happened, an interruption or event has occurred that has an impact on the work process and/or relationships. A decision as to what type of conversation is needed next is critical at this juncture.

Source: Adapted from Newfield Network, Inc.

process items; task assignments are made, resources are allocated, quality standards are established, and due dates are set. Think about times when you left an action conversation, clearly focused and motivated toward action. Coming full circle from speculative to action conversation is vital to ensure that execution happens.

Let's continue with the example of Kim. She utilized fun, speculative conversations to gather ideas and options. Then to make something happen, to take the next steps, she conducted a well-timed action meeting. This meeting had a more focused agenda, which enabled the participants to make decisions from all the possible choices contributed. People volunteered for some assignments. Other tasks were delegated. Everyone knew exactly which action to take, which new direction to pursue, and which target dates to meet for completion. Kim's action conversation sets her team into motion.

Another action conversation that often needs to take place deals with communication breakdowns. Any type of breakdown must be handled as soon as possible. Conversations about breakdowns require decisive action that squarely addresses the situation. The immediacy of managing breakdowns minimizes their impact, contains losses, and allows your team to quickly refocus and redirect resources and energy.

Kim's strategy for handling communication breakdowns is to keep in constant contact with her team. She effectively delegates, avoiding any micromanaging, and she is approachable when problems occur. She uses a full range of communication devices to keep everyone in the loop on the project's status. She facilitates individual and group coaching sessions to address situations stemming from the more delicate people issues that emerge. Breakdowns are seen as a natural function of any project and are utilized as learning experiences. They are part of the developmental process Kim has for growing her team individually and collectively, and encouraging communication mastery.

Community-building conversations include orientation and trust conversations. Both are conversations that help to forge relationships and shape the culture of the organization (table 6-3). *Orientation conversations* often occur at the onset of a new position, role, or job. These are critical because they establish the framework within which everyone in the organization will operate. For new hires, orientation conversations tell your company's story, complete with its heroes and memorable moments. One of the most famous of these is the "Traditions" course required for all new Disney employees. Positive attitudes can be enhanced through repeated orientation conversations, like departmental meetings, retreats, and companywide events. Project orientation conversations are often called kick-off meetings. In these conversations, your goals and expectations for the project are reinforced so that all members of your team know who is doing what, when, and how.

Kim manages orientation conversations by sending weekly updates on the project, along with progress reports of accomplished goals. She acts as cheerleader when the team meets both major and modest milestones. In addition, she maintains high visibility, increasing the opportunity for her team to approach her with issues that could potentially derail the project and damage the trust established among the group.

> *The right conversation in the wrong mood is the wrong conversation.*
>
> —Julio Olalla

Trust conversations bring people together, especially when a breakdown occurs that could potentially damage relationships. No item is too small to be addressed. When

Table 6-3. Community-Building Conversations

Type of Conversation	Distinctions
Orientation conversations	Conversations that build and create the group's story give shared meaning to events. It is here that connections are made between the individual and the organization.
Trust conversations	Conversations can build and enable trusting relationships. Solid relationships support joint actions. Complaints and issues that have potential to damage relationships are addressed openly.

Source: Adapted from Newfield Network, Inc.

a team member has an issue, address it openly with everyone involved. Often a solution is evident, sometimes something as simple as an apology or explanation. There may be times when no solution is possible and the people part ways, agreeing to disagree. Regardless of the outcome, people must be treated with respect and dignity. Others are watching! Trust conversations are critical to the success of any team, of every company.

There is another type of trust conversation. These are the private conversations that you, as the manager, hold in confidence and conduct with care—performance reviews, professional development discussions, and any conversations about personal issues. Performance evaluations require a delicate touch. In conducting them, you focus on actions and behaviors. You offer evidence to increase shared understanding and specific insights to grow your employee and further a trusting relationship. Being prepared is the best way to make those often uncomfortable professional development conversations easier and more productive. Preparation will help you find the best way to share blind spots or performance changes so that they will be heard and appreciated as information points to help someone grow. Conversations about personal issues must be conducted discreetly, objectively, and with a selfless agenda. Savvy managers know that no one action can do more damage to their working relationship than breaching trust on any confidential matter.

Creating the space for the right type of conversation to fully develop can be considered an exceptional talent. It brings together many of the process ideas we are sharing with you. Before you take part in any conversation, be clear about what you really want as an outcome for yourself and others. Remember, it is the right conversation that will drive actions to your desired outcomes.

Savvy Translation: Savvy managers recognize that different types of conversations serve different purposes. They strategically use the right conversation to achieve their desired outcome and appropriately label conversations for greater clarity.

Focused Listening

What do you listen? Yes, this is purposely phrased in an awkward manner. This very important question asks you to recognize exactly what holds your attention as you listen when someone speaks. Learning to listen and truly connecting with another person are a rare and highly desirable competency. It all starts with you becoming more aware of what affects your listening. Through self-management, you learn to give your full attention to another person. You listen to more than the words, working to discern underlying concerns that are being expressed. This practice lets you connect with and validate the speaker. It is the essence of focused listening.

> *The greatest motivational act*
> *one person can do for another*
> *is to listen.*
>
> —Roy E. Moody

Focused listening targets all your senses on the speaker. You not only listen to the words being said, but you also focus on shades of meaning. You are attuned to the speaker's emotional domain. You observe body movements and reflect on the behaviors and vocal expressions you observe. You identify the motivations behind what the speaker is saying and establish your assumptions around why it is being said. As the conversation unfolds, you test the accuracy of any assumptions you make. You make adjustments for the context around the conversation, recognizing what is happening within the environment and around the situation, providing a space or frame for what you are hearing. Savvy managers know that "waiting to talk" is not the same thing as listening.

Your listening is deeply embedded in your perceptions. Listening is always a filtered interpretation of what is being heard by your inner observer who sees the world and events in a certain way. This process of filtering information guides your actions, aligning not only how you see the world but also how you hear the world. Listening is clearly connected to the visual images you form as you listen. It is critical for you to understand that all listening is interpreted listening. You need to realize that your interpretation can be right or wrong; it can be objective or subjective, accurate or inaccurate. The key point here is that it is *yours*. And, just as you want people to acknowledge your interpretation, you must learn to accept the interpretations of others. Legitimacy does not mean agreement, but it does create the place where the parties involved can move forward in effective conversation.

There are additional considerations that have an impact on your listening. Your relationship with the speaker will likely affect how you listen. For example, if you admire and respect the person speaking, your listening will be highly focused. The reverse is also true. When you believe you are the smartest person in the room, the only one who really knows what's happening, the ace with all the answers, your listening is compromised before anyone utters a word. Also, as Ken Wilber showed us in chapter 3, the internal collective prism might be operating here. There could be experiences and a history within which the person is speaking and you are listening. The emotional field being triggered while you listen can either open or close your listening. Your own skill to listen at another level is a consideration in how well you can uncover the genuine and unspoken concerns of the speaker.

Improving your listening capabilities takes practice. The good news is that you have opportunities to practice every day. Developing each one of four key skills presented in table 6-4 will significantly enhance your listening skills. Mastery will heighten your ability to offer clear responses that are insightful and relevant to the issues at hand. It is the exceptional and gifted listener who seeks first to fully and completely understand the speaker. As a manager and leader, developing your ability to truly listen offers you intimate connections with people that are beyond measure.

The Power of Language

Inherent in every effective conversation is your ability to use language. Language, that mutually agreed upon shared code where meaning is assigned, has the ability to transform. Your words and the intention directing them create your world and your results. What you say has the power to do good and the power to destroy. When you

Table 6-4. Four Key Listening Skills

Skill	Savvy Listening Strategies
Focus your attention.	Stop multitasking and focus your attention. Really listen, allowing the words and meaning to enter your mind without inner argument. Replay key words in your head while you study tone, mood, and body movement. Avoid beginning your counterarguments or mentally listing any objections. Just listen.
Distinguish the speaker's real motive and/or action.	Stay in the space of the attentive listener until the speaker is completely finished. Get clear if any actions are warranted. If the motive is only a desire for someone to truly listen, be silent and still and really listen. Wait to uncover what action, if any, you might take. The speaker will let you know.
Consider the context.	Place your conversation in the right contextual environment. Identify the situational issues and external factors causing the speaker to express what you are hearing. Ask questions to clarify your thoughts about context and meaning.
Question at a deeper level.	Grow your ability to go deeper. Explore the full range of interpretations of what is being expressed. Let go of your own perceptual responses. Listening is about the speaker, not you! Invest the time and illuminate concerns to add clarity to what is being said.

speak with clearly articulated positive thoughts and ideas, you can inspire and empower people to produce results. Using affirming language with your employees changes the dynamics of the environment and strengthens the relationship. It leads to more solid, higher-quality performances, which increase the organization's profitability. However, when you address people from the heat of an emotional field, you can damage relationships. When you discount people, disrespecting them through what you say and how you say it, their participation and commitment to the work dissolve. Language helps to create sustainable change. It is critical that you realize that language is not innocent (Olalla 2000).

> *Words carry their own kind of energy.*
> —Maya Angelou

Speech Act Theory

Because language is the primary mode through which you coordinate your actions with others, it is important to learn exactly how to best use language to accomplish your goals. Think of conversations as interlocking and related networks of language. There is a purpose and a future desired state embedded within every conversation. There are actions and consequences, interpretations and assessments, commitments and breakdowns. To truly build your conversational competence and communication power, you must be able to leverage the pattern or flow of the conversation itself. Consider this proposition: When you speak, there are only five broad categories of action used. These are called speech acts (Olalla 2000).

Speech acts are simply defined as the building blocks of conversations. And, putting these blocks together to make conversation is something that you've been doing since you first started talking. Your coaching here is to make speech acts accessible as a process tool. This will enable you to learn when and how to use each act to improve your conversational competence. Table 6-5 summarizes the five speech acts with a simple description and gives an example of each. Explore the table with three purposes in mind. First, seek to understand the function of each speech act. Second, examine how you currently use (or do not use) each speech act. And finally, experiment with speech acts more intentionally as you build conversations.

To leverage speech act theory to its full advantage, there are five important points to consider. First, speech acts clarify the intention of a conversation. You need to recognize your intention and focus your conversation to give power to it. Second, each of us comes to any conversation from our own emotional context. Incorporating

Table 6-5. Speech Acts

Speech Act	Description	Examples
Assertion	Factual statements that other people can easily verify, witness, or find evidence to show as true or false.	Susan works 10-hour days. Joe starts work at 6:00 p.m. on Mondays.
Declaration	Statements made that change reality. The person making the declaration must have the authority to make it. There are four different types of declarations: beginning declarations; ending declarations; resolving declarations; and assessments, which are declarations of your opinion.	Beginning declaration: You are hired. Ending declaration: You are fired. Resolving declaration: Joe will be on the committee, not John. Assessment: Sue performs better than Ed.
Request	Asking for something that is missing or needed. Requests may be formatted as questions, suggestions, propositions, orders, demands, or invitations.	May I have the data analysis? You are invited to the party. Get me the Sloan report.
Offer	Volunteering your services or taking action to satisfy a need or concern. Offers include things that you can skillfully do, as well as just being the person you are.	I can prepare the slides for your presentation. Gloria, as a unique person, in and of herself is an offer.
Commitment	Promise to do something that you keep. Must be able to answer both "yes" and "no."	I will meet you at 10:00 a.m. The project will be finished on Monday.

Source: Adapted from Newfield Network, Inc.

speech acts into your conversations enables you to better handle the emotional fields. Asking for information is less threatening than directly challenging an assessment. Making a request for someone to accept responsibility for a task is more effective than handing out assignments.

Third, both requests and offers need to be made in a complete manner, leaving nothing to chance or misinterpretation. There must be both a speaker and a committed listener. The speaker identifies a need or something that is missing and required in a situation. The speaker states the action desired, so no one is guessing about what must be done. A timeframe and results that will satisfy the need are also clearly stated. Any additional information required to complete the task is provided, and someone accepts the request.

Fourth, one of the most powerful declarations is called an *assessment*. These are statements of judgment, standards, or evaluation. Unlike assertions, which can be true or false, assessments can be valid or invalid. They are made in the present, based on a past perception, and predict a possible future. The key words to highlight in this definition are "perception" and "possible." Because assessments are not true or false facts, the savvy manager recognizes an assessment when one is offered, and then works to validate it or change it (Olalla 2000).

Here is an example of how to handle an assessment. You have just heard from another project manager that Jerry, a new addition to your project team, does shoddy work. Before you accept this assessment of Jerry's work habits as fact, you act consciously and choose to get more information. You recognize that you need to know more about his circumstances, and you wisely decide to go straight to the source. You invite Jerry for coffee before your first team meeting. The unknown you discover is that Jerry has been overloaded with high-priority tasks from his boss. He admits to being the type of guy who just takes them all and does the best he can.

You now have facts that discredit the earlier assessment and create a new picture of Jerry's work. You recognize that Jerry has a strong work ethic, will bring specific talents to your project team, and needs help learning to say "no" to authority figures. As this simple example shows, assessments held as facts, without validation, can be dangerous. Savvy managers always seek out supportive evidence about the assessments they hold. Ask yourself this coaching question before we move on: *How many assessments are you holding right now as facts?*

> *Words are, of course, the most powerful drug used by mankind.*
> —Rudyard Kipling

Finally, making and keeping commitments strengthens your relationships with others. Your ability to keep the commitments you make is a higher-order adult skill, part of your process of evolving. This means that you will say "no" to a request to which you cannot fully commit, regardless of the reason. Your "no" in the workplace does not necessarily mean forever. It may simply mean that you cannot commit now but could fulfill the request for a project or task at a later date. "No" often begins negotiations. It can also illuminate a problem that lies below the surface, one perceived as a taboo topic. When you are not allowed to say "no" to a request, commitment becomes compliance. At this point, your required "yes" will be a lie that compromises your integrity. The savvy manager truly recognizes that commitment is the only successful course to follow. "No" to unethical, immoral, or dishonest requests is always "no."

Incorporating the building blocks of speech acts into your conversations connects directly to the savvy skills of acting consciously, collaborating, and evolving. Initially, it will take a concerted effort to identify which speech acts will be most effective as process tools in your interactions. As you utilize them, you will increase the effectiveness of your conversations and your ability to coordinate your actions with others. You will think more quickly and confidently, and better observe what is going on in real time. You will learn how to make requests, present offers, and clearly declare your

> *To be human is to be the kind of being that generates commitments through speaking and listening. Without our ability to create and accept (or decline) commitments, we are acting in a less than fully human way, and we are not fully using language.*
>
> —Terry Winograd
> and Fernando Flores

intentions. You will discover the power behind making commitments and keeping them. And you will gain confidence and grow your personal power every time you keep your commitments.

Savvy Translation: Savvy managers recognize the power of language. They use speech intelligently to create conversations that produce the desired outcomes. They welcome "no" as an expression of personal dignity and an opportunity to build trust.

The Bottom Line: Mastering Communication

The conversations in today's workplace are taking place among very diverse human beings as they try hard to coordinate their ongoing actions with one another. The end goal is to bring out the best performance in each person. Beyond the basics of human communication, the challenge is really to become an expert communicator in a way that invites the honest interplay of thoughts and ideas, moves forward the actions of all involved, and propels your company to sustainable profitability. Developing your capabilities lets you have open and honest conversations. You find ease in handling emotionally charged, risk-intense, often controversial issues. When you integrate basic elements like purpose, language, speech acts, and dialogue into a conversation, meaningful communication occurs. Creating collaborative conversations, where the challenge is focused on finding solutions to complex problems, engages everyone.

The tools and techniques offered here take practice. First, you must be conscious of the elements of dialogue and how to incorporate speech acts. You must self-manage and encourage actions that move the conversations forward in your desired direction. And yes, you must intentionally eliminate any jibes and offhand comments that inhibit full participation from others. You must practice focused listening, stop multitasking, and learn to reflect on conversations that have occurred. With practice, these process tools will become habits, and you will wonder how you ever lived without them.

Use It or Lose It

Write down the one key idea that you "got" as a takeaway from your reading. Then write down what you plan to do starting tomorrow to integrate this idea, practice it, and make it a habit.

1. What I got. _____
   _____

2. How I will use it tomorrow. _____
   _____

3. Which savvy skill(s) I am developing. _____
   _____

Reflection Interval

Communication is the essence of what we each do intimately with ourselves and outwardly with others. As you have read, it emanates from how we hold ourselves, which then leads to how we express our thoughts to others. The story below shines a light on how a small group of people learned to hold themselves as gifts to the world. How can you apply this same principle to your own life?

The Rabbi's Gift

Use with permission from Jerry Hampton

The story concerns a monastery that had fallen upon hard times. It was once a great order, but because of persecution, all its branch houses were lost, and there were only five monks left in the decaying house: the abbot and four others, all over seventy in age. Clearly it was a dying order.

In the deep woods surrounding the monastery, there was a little hut that a rabbi occasionally used for a hermitage. The old monks had become a bit psychic, so they could always sense when the rabbi was in his hermitage. "The rabbi is in the woods, the rabbi is in the woods," they would whisper. It occurred to the abbot that a visit with the rabbi might result in some advice to save his monastery.

The rabbi welcomed the abbot to his hut. But when the abbot explained his visit, the rabbi could only say, "I know how it is. The spirit has gone out of the people. It is the same in my town. Almost no one comes to the synagogue anymore." So the old abbot and the old rabbi wept together. Then they read parts of the Torah and spoke of deep things. When the abbot had to leave, they embraced each other. "It has been wonderful that we should meet after all these years," the abbot said, "but I have failed in my purpose for coming here. Is there nothing you can tell me that would help me save my dying order?"

"No, I am sorry," the rabbi responded. "I have no advice to give. But, I can tell you that the Messiah is one of you."

When the abbot returned to the monastery, his fellow monks gathered around him to ask, "Well, what did the rabbi say?"

"The rabbi said something very mysterious; it was something cryptic. He said that the Messiah is one of us. I don't know what he meant."

In the time that followed, the old monks wondered whether there was significance to the rabbi's words. The Messiah is one of us? Could he possibly have meant one of us monks? If so, which one? Do you suppose he meant the abbot? Yes, if he meant anyone, he probably meant Father Abbot. He has been our leader for more than a generation. On the other hand, he might have meant Brother Thomas. Certainly Brother Thomas is a holy man. Everyone knows that Thomas is a man of light. Certainly he could not have meant Brother Elred! Elred gets crotchety at times. But come to think of it, even though he is a thorn in people's sides, when you look back on it, Elred is virtually always right. Often very right. Maybe the rabbi did mean Brother Elred. But surely not Brother Phillip. Phillip is so passive, a real nobody. But then, almost mysteriously, he has a gift for always being there when you need him. He just magically appears. Maybe Phillip is the Messiah.

Of course the rabbi didn't mean me. He couldn't possibly have meant me. I'm just an ordinary person. Yet supposing he did? Suppose I am the Messiah? O God, not me. I couldn't be that much for You, could I?

As they contemplated, the old monks began to treat each other with extraordinary respect on the chance that one among them might be the Messiah. And they began to treat themselves with extraordinary respect.

People still occasionally came to visit the monastery in its beautiful forest to picnic on its tiny lawn, to wander along some of its paths, even to meditate in the dilapidated chapel. As they did so, they sensed the aura of extraordinary respect that began to surround the five old monks and seemed to radiate out from them and permeate the atmosphere of the place. There was something strangely compelling about it. Hardly knowing why, they began to come back to the monastery to picnic, to play, to pray. They brought their friends to this special place. And their friends brought their friends.

Then some of the younger men who came to visit the monastery started to talk more and more with the old monks. After a while, one asked if he could join them. Then another, and another. So within a few years, the monastery had once again become a thriving order and, thanks to the rabbi's gift, a vibrant center of light and spirituality in the realm.

Coaching for Action: Driving Optimal Performance
Reflective Communication Questions

Assess your own effectiveness as a communicator. Think about each of the following questions and how you might become a more effective communicator.

Igniting effective conversation:
1. How does conversation make people more effective?
2. If you believe there is an important conversation that needs to take place at work, how can you bring it into being?

Supporting dialogue:
1. How do you create the space for dialogue?
2. How do engage in conversations that generate possibilities for all involved?

Practicing Speech Acts

To incorporate speech acts into your conversations, take one speech act and begin to consciously use it every chance you get. We suggest you start with requests, as these are the easiest to notice and change.
1. During the first week, notice how many effective requests you can make. Keep a record of each request and the results you get. Are your requests being made in a way that produces the outcomes you want?
2. During the second week, make a concerted effort to include the different elements of an effective request that you read about on pages 100–102. These include having a committed listener, identifying the need or missing item, stating the required action desired, setting time frames, satisfying results profile, providing all necessary information to complete the task, and acknowledging acceptance of the request.

3. Select a different speech act beginning week three. Follow the same process. Keep notes on what you say and notice the results you get. What do you observe about the power behind speech acts?

Lagniappe

Communication is the essence of human interaction. As you grow your savvy, you expand your capacity to effectively interact with your employees and produce better results. Visit the Learning Annex 4 at www.astd.org/SavvyManager. Review "Communication Basics." Pay attention to the new communication courtesies required by advances in technology. Use the "Fundamentals of Listening" in Learning Annex 5 as your guide for building your listening competency.

Harnessing Enlightened Power

It's not a question of how much power you can hoard for yourself but how much you can give away.

—Benjamin Zander

Build your savvy as you learn to

- identify power as energy, not force
- cultivate *enlightened power* and apply it in the workplace
- utilize influence and relationship strategies to effectively lead and manage
- establish a culture of empowerment throughout your organization

Dictionaries define power using phrases like "act or perform effectively," "strength or force exerted," and "official capacity to exert control." Power is a force you apply. We believe that effectively managing in today's highly interdependent organizations means using power to produce results that serve the diverse needs of all stakeholders. We are offering a fresh interpretation of power as *energy* rather than force. This deeper understanding opens the door to connect to what we are labeling your enlightened power source. To set the stage for our exploration of enlightened power, we first make distinctions about what most people think of when they talk about power.

■ ■ ■

Real Time: Whitney's Story

I was reading a bedtime story to my son the other night and chuckled to myself thinking how politically incorrect it was. It was interesting to see the power struggles and how good and evil showed up among the different characters. This got me thinking about my own leadership team, the way each person uses power, and how differently they manage. If ever there was an "evil stepsister" lurking around, it was inside of Gayle, our director of sales. I remember all those talks I had with her about her approach to managing her sales team.

When she was first promoted, Gayle was overbearing with everyone, myself included. She was always working from her titled position. Everything from voice mail to memos was signed from "the director of sales." It was irritating, especially to her peers. Our culture here has always been more relaxed and flexible. None of us were ever caught up in our titles.

Then something changed. It was almost like the Fairy Godmother paid her a visit one night! I knew Gayle was always reading business books because she was constantly parroting current management fads to everyone. Somewhere along the way, her reading connected with her actions, and she started incorporating those strategies with her group. She began to walk her talk! Her transformation was amazing, and the company has really benefited. I'd love to see that happen for everyone.

Gayle seems to have found her magic. She is more astute about using her power to create the results she really wants. She really looks for ways to connect with the customers we serve. I admire her ability to handle the pressure with such poise and diplomacy. While the old Gayle would have barked orders or shut down and stalked off angrily, the new Gayle is responding appropriately, speaking freely, sharing her insights and wisdom, and inviting others to do the same. Gayle's been great at defusing the tensions and posturing of her sales team, getting them focused on solving problems instead of creating new ones. And that's no easy job with her sales team. They are highly competitive, ego-driven people.

Just as Gayle has done, I need to help all my managers connect to their own power. Using power wisely is the ultimate learning for anyone who manages. It is so easy to get off on a power trip and foolishly think you really are in charge. I know that helping each of them feel empowered is part of my accountability as the manager. I just need to find that right "something" to make this happen for all of us! Hello, Fairy Godmother, I need you here!

■ ■ ■

Legitimate power comes from a designated position, station, or role that one holds within an organization, a division of a company, or even a family or social group. The president of the United States, the pope, and the queen of England all have positional power by virtue of their given role and title. Clearly, the persona of the people holding each of the positions plays a part, too. Over time, presidents, popes, and royalty have exemplified both the best and worst of each position.

Enter authority. In your assigned position as manager, you have authority and legitimate power to make things happen in a prescribed manner to produce the results you want. You have accountability to establish plans and delegate duties, and the authority to see that work is completed to your satisfaction. You evaluate performances and recommend promotions and raises. You may personally hire and fire, reward, and/or punish employees. How you use your authority from your position as manager links to your management and leadership style and determines the relationship that develops between yourself and your employees.

> *Power is the capacity to ensure the outcomes one wishes and to prevent those one does not wish.*
> —John W. Gardner

Enlightened power, separate and distinct from authority or positional power, can be developed by anyone, regardless of his or her place in the pecking order within the organization. We want you to dig deep into your core to really understand those personal attributes that contribute to developing your own enlightened power. Enlightened power emanates from you, as an individual who takes action in concert with your core qualities and your deeply held values about other human beings. This is power to which others will respond because it honors them. Your coaching in this chapter focuses on helping you connect to a power that is stronger than what you might have ever considered is available to you.

We want you to realize the contextual arena of power in your organization and just how influence connects to power and empowerment, for yourself and your team. This learning also allows you to be more astute when confronted with power plays from others. Through our discussion, you will come to realize that the heart of enlightened power beats through the integration of the savvy skills of self-managing, reflecting, and acting consciously. You evolve. As people respond to your authenticity, you effectively leverage your energy to get things done

> *The safest person to give power to is the one who doesn't enjoy power.*
> —Abraham Maslow

the *right* way. And just what is the right way to use power? Your real power flows from understanding exactly how you influence, change, inspire, and obtain results that benefit the many, without harm to any. This is what we regard as the *right* way to utilize power as a savvy manager.

The Power Dynamic

Julio Olalla (2000) tells us that power is a mental construct based on a relationship that exists in a context. It functions uniquely in each environment and stems from how you and others relate with one another. It is invisible energy. Imagine it as a pulse of energy moving along a continuum. In and of itself, power is neither good nor bad. Rather, it is the use or absence of power that explains its force and impact for each situation. Consider just how the power dynamic shows up in these scenarios:

- Judy complains that she is stressed because her boss is demeaning and abrupt. She tells everyone that he is making her life miserable but, because he's the boss, there is nothing she can do.
- Richard is a regional vice president for the bank. He functions as a leader with his immediate team, inspiring them to produce results. However, during board meetings, he is reticent and hesitates to share his thoughts and ideas. His strength as a leader seems to disappear in the presence of his superiors.
- Darlene is the administrative assistant to the company CEO. Because she is engaging and welcoming with everyone, she is continually approached for insight and direction on a wide range of projects and issues. Her influence seems to extend well beyond that of a traditional administrative assistant.

The dynamics of power in each of these examples reveals itself uniquely for each person through the various relationships and within each different circumstance. For Judy and Richard, inaction follows their feelings about their power in certain situations. Darlene, however, leverages her own personal power beyond what her position might normally hold.

These examples may speak to your own power dynamic. Reconsider the energy pulse image. As you imagine it moving back and forth, growing larger or smaller, evaluate the power that others have over you. Assess what power you might hold over them. Determine when their pulse is large or small and just how yours compares. Your perceptions of the interplay of power form your assessments about what your power allows you to do, and what it helps you to get. Power grows, recedes, or stays solid as it travels along the dynamic from you to another, or from someone else to you. It is your power belief, your story of how powerful you are, that directs you to take or refrain from taking action.

Your mental construct about power becomes your gauge for actions. You must routinely test your perceptions about your own power, and the power you feel others hold. Whenever you *think* that someone has more power than

> *Real power: the ability to make the impossible possible—effortlessly!*
> —Anonymous

you, you can easily lose your sense of purpose and desire to act. Try playing the mind game that asks you to think about the worst that could happen. *How would you cope?* If you are thinking that you are powerless, unable to cope with a particular chain of events, then you likely have given away your real power. When you have developed coping strategies that allow you to see other options, your internal power is present and strong. Stop and reflect in every situation where power is at play. You always have the power to reshape your thoughts and find new alternatives for every situation in your life!

Another important dynamic of power flows from the strength of relationships. As we have discussed, the success of any relationship lives in the emotional domain of the individuals involved. And although the rational business world cautions you to separate emotions in your professional dealings, emotions are at the heart of power and the linchpin of your actions. As human beings, we react or respond based on our perceptions and how we *feel* toward one another. Embedded in your feelings (love, hate, fear, respect, and the like) is a belief in the power that exists in that relationship. This belief is key in creating the energy or power that drives your interactions with that person to create the power dynamic.

Think about colleagues and managers with whom you have worked. Consider the feelings that emerge when interacting with a manager who intimidates you with threats or disgusts you with inappropriate humor. Compare those with your feelings about a manager who treats the building maintenance workers with the same thoughtfulness and consideration as the company president. Look at the positive feelings that occur when employees extend the same outstanding customer service to each other as they do to external clients. Compare it with the relationships that arise when they don't. The feelings that support the interpersonal relationships exhibited in these examples either damage or enhance the power of each person taking action. Wheatley (1992, 38–39) clearly identifies the connection:

> Power in organizations is the capacity generated by relationships...
> power is energy; it needs to flow through organizations; it cannot be con-
> fined to functions or levels.... What gives power its charge, positive or
> negative, is the quality of relationships. Those you relate to through coer-
> cion, or from a disregard for the other person, create negative energy.
> Those who are open to others and who see others in their fullness create
> positive energy.

The savvy manager fully understands the power dynamic with all its subtle permu-
tations. Through enlightened power, you understand people in a deeper way. You
fully appreciate how your own needs and wants connect to what others need and
want. Enlightened power evolves beyond position or dominance. It is the highest
form of attraction energy. Others are drawn to you; your authenticity is very real.
People with enlightened power respect and honor everyone. They are self-aware, they
self-manage, and they use a collaborative spirit to bring out the best in everyone.
They only take action in ways that are consistent with everyone maintaining his or
her personal dignity. Someone with enlightened power is the epitome of strength
with a true and genuine soul. These people can move mountains!

 Savvy Translation: Savvy managers know that their real power is only
a function of the level of authority and respect afforded to them by others. They rely on influence and relationships, not dominance or control,
to get results.

Connecting to Enlightened Power

Savvy managers are grounded in a way that gives them the confidence to act from
strength and not ego. From this place, they can easily bring out the best in themselves and others. Unlike dominance and control *over* other people, enlightened
power emanates from within. It is *real* power that manifests from your own sense of
self-worth as a fully functioning adult. It moves beyond the illusion of control over
another to keen insightfulness of per-
sonal feelings and conscious actions. You
truly know yourself and are comfortable
with who you are. There is no drive or
need to constantly prove yourself. This
opens the door to actions that you
might otherwise believe are beneath you
or outside the scope of your duties as a

> *Treat people as if they were*
> *what they ought to be and you*
> *help them to become what they*
> *are capable of being.*
>
> —Johann Wolfgang von Goethe

manager. You become fully aware of how every interaction enables or diminishes your power. What you learn is that the more cohesively you align your thoughts, feelings, and actions, the larger your real power arena becomes.

Dr. Al has a small medical practice where enlightened power lives. When he heard an angry patient using profanity with his administrative staff over a billing issue, he pulled the patient aside and privately told him that such behavior was inappropriate and unacceptable. He quietly explained that personal dignity was extended *to all, by all* in his office. While acknowledging that the patient was upset, Dr. Al requested that he still respect his staff and curtail his abusive language. Dr. Al informed the patient that if this would not be possible, then the patient's medical records would be sent to another physician of his choosing. In this example, Dr. Al used his power to ensure that everyone was treated with dignity. He could have ignored what was happening at his front desk. He could have let his staff deal with the patient. He chose a different path. His actions upheld his personal values about how *all* people get treated. His staff responded, as did the patient, and they worked together to address the billing issue.

Think about managers to whom you have reported, as well as others you have seen in action. It is an amazing sight to watch them smoothly defuse a belligerent, angry customer and convert him or her into a calm, satisfied one. It is motivating to witness a manager move into action to support his or her employees by doing just what needs to be done in that moment. It's the little things that managers do that make the biggest difference. They will get a mop to clean a spill, open another register or bag merchandise, or make coffee for clients and staff. All these things show managers rising above rank and moving past the words of a job description. It also shows a manager willing to *be* with employees—not watching from the sidelines. This manager uses his or her real power to marshal energy toward action, thereby expanding everyone's capacity to produce results. And all this is accomplished without ever casting aspersions or destroying the power of another person.

Developing enlightened power requires you to be clear about your values and honor them in all of your interactions. Examine the skills described in table 7-1 that we claim are essential to acquiring your own enlightened power. The savvy translations in the table will help you apply these skills in your workplace. Assess your own ability to practice these simple skills consistently. Recall people with whom you work who exhibit these skills, as well as those who do not. In the final analysis, reflecting gives you 20/20 hindsight about what you "should have, could have, wish you would have done" that can become great foresight. As you learn how to harness your own real power, you become a role model for others on your team to emulate.

Table 7-1. Enlightened Power: Your Real Power

Process Skill	Conceptual Focus	Savvy Translation
Self-awareness	You know who you are at a deep, insightful place, and you are comfortable with this person. Your comfort enables actions that are driven by a true desire for everyone to become his or her best, rather than by your own self-aggrandizement.	Savvy managers ask themselves insightful questions that reveal the reasons behind their feelings and actions. They know that everything they do, think, and say comes from within. They see encounters as opportunities for growth. They feel no need to prove their self-worth.
Observing, being aware	You are aware of things that happen around you. You practice the role of observer to see beyond what is apparent.	Savvy managers know that what they observe is only part of what is really happening. They pay attention to all the things in their world that affect them. This allows them to take more effective and appropriate actions when necessary.
Keeping commitments	You keep your word to yourself and to others. Because you recognize exactly what it means to make and keep your word, you refrain from making promises that you can't make every effort to keep.	Savvy managers know that keeping commitments is the cornerstone of enlightened power. They establish new behaviors for making and keeping promises and their integrity thrives. They know that their real power links to that place of integrity where words match behavior, especially when no one is watching. They acknowledge broken commitments and renegotiate for mutual satisfaction.
Being accountable	You are accountable for the actions you choose to take and the results you obtain from those actions. You have ownership of your life.	Savvy managers take full ownership for things that happen in their lives. They act consciously and accept the risks/rewards of their choices. They never blame anyone for anything. Others respect and admire the ability they have to hold themselves accountable, and are attracted by this high level of personal ownership.
Speaking the truth	You speak the truth in all things, recognizing that it is only your truth. You then listen while others share their truth, which opens the space for real power to flow from everyone.	Savvy managers tell the truth to themselves and others. They listen with an open mind. With kindness, respect, and diplomacy, they use the power of truth to direct and help others to grow.
Making requests	You ask for what you want. You are sufficiently clear and purposeful to be heard.	Savvy managers know how to effectively communicate genuine requests. They use their requests to show what is most important and keep everyone focused on the goal. They allow others to accept or decline offers and use that insight to choose new requests.

Because making and keeping your commitments is a critical aspect of enlightened power, a few additional comments about this important and very difficult skill are warranted. Think about the promises you make—the small things you say you will do but never actually carry out. Extend this thought to the ramifications of not following through: the phone call you didn't return before noon as you said you would, or the report that didn't make it to your boss by the end of the day as promised. On the surface, these examples may seem to be merely communication issues, but your real power is diminished in each situation because trust has been violated. Someone on the receiving end of your commitment believed you and now has to compensate for your failure to deliver.

There are also the personal commitments you make to yourself. Things like eating and living healthily, exercising, or spending more quality time with your families and friends are easy to say and hard to deliver. These small, broken personal commitments can make you stop believing in yourself as someone who delivers on promises. Failure to keep these simple commitments chips away at your real power. You lose some of your power with every commitment you neglect to keep to yourself and others.

> *When you do not seek or need external approval, you are at your most powerful.*
> —Carolyn Myss

In the final analysis, power is yours to maintain or to lose. A little piece of yourself is expanded every time you use your power effectively and is slightly diminished whenever you give away your power. You hear people saying things like "He makes me mad!" or "She hurt my feelings" or "They should know without me having to ask." When you speak this way, you are saying that you have no power over your feelings or actions—that others are in control. Nothing could be further from the truth. Yes, someone can say hurtful things. How you react or respond is totally up to you; you are accountable. Similarly, you feel your real power when you get what you want because you expressed a need and asked for it. Practice the language of power that says *I want. I am. I choose. I will!* Look first at yourself for answers about power.

 Savvy Translation: Savvy managers know that power is a mental construct. They believe in their own enlightened power, which is born of strength—not ego. They harness this power to act in concert with the organization's vision and values to produce outcomes that exceed expectations.

The Empowerment Zone

Empowerment—authorizing and extending power to another—represents an enigma. The ideas of commitment, decision-making responsibility, contribution, and autonomy always sound great and look so good on paper. Both management and employees claim they want empowerment in the workplace. Organizations pursue empowered employees who will think, solve problems, take smart risks, and assume accountability. Employees are looking for environments in which to become active, contributing members where collaboration prevails and where issues are addressed in a forthright manner that excludes blame and fault finding. And yet for many reasons, most managers hesitate taking the intentional actions required to make empowerment the culture that produces greater performance and productivity.

> *Power can be taken but not given.*
> *The process of the taking is*
> *empowerment in itself.*
> —Gloria Steinem

Empowerment is not a program or a single process. Rather, it is part of the foundational culture that you establish in your organization. It is embedded in all interactions, clearly articulated through every communication, and supported by management practices. This means that employees are given and accept accountability for their work, and that management supports and encourages them.

The "em" prefix in "empower" sets the context. To feel and experience power *from within* is the essence of this concept. Empowerment requires that the employee be committed to the vision of the organization or the project. That commitment directly connects to the required level of personal ownership of the outcomes produced. It is a commitment that extends far beyond the concept of "pay for work." It is supported by both focused intentions and the often-unexpressed intrinsic motivators that drive committed performance.

Empowerment is more than just changing the perception of who has power or of claiming that employees have been given power. It is about helping individuals empower themselves by fully realizing and utilizing their enlightened power. Your coaching here is about shifting the underlying attitudes, beliefs, and values that you (as management) and your employees hold about one another. Making empowerment more than an elusive term takes the combined energies of every member of the team. Empowerment illuminates mutual trust.

Coaching for You, the Manager

Creating an empowered workforce takes time and requires a deep commitment on everyone's part. As the manager, it is your job to establish the context where empowered employees can thrive. You define what empowerment really means in the concrete terms of their daily activities. You set the expectations and describe how outcomes will be measured. You foster the image of success with every employee so that each person can construct his or her belief system around that image. Each element—mental construct, relationship, and context—furthers your distinctions and the growth of your enlightened power.

Taking these elements a step further, you communicate the vision and goals of the organization to clearly define the parameters for all actions from your employees. You serve as a resource, teacher, mentor, and coach. You forfeit your hero role and allow your people to become problem solvers. You encourage them to think critically and creatively and use you as a sounding board rather than as the provider of answers. You support decisions and actions from your empowered employees. Your unconditional support boosts their confidence and the sense of ownership and accountability that accompanies empowerment. You conduct follow-up action meetings and debriefings to evaluate results. You offer feedback to employees, always establishing the contexts for these sessions as opportunities to enhance future performance. As the manager, you recognize when commands are needed and provide essential direction. Likewise, you know when to step back and open the space for autonomous action.

> *We have learned that power is a positive force if it is used for positive purposes.*
> —Elizabeth Dole

Hannah always speaks of creating an empowered workforce. She tells the members of her team she wants them to challenge her, take risks, and find new ways to grow the business. It all sounds good, and it works smoothly until she is challenged on an issue she doesn't want to discuss. When people act in a way that she thinks is outside their bounds, she quickly calls them to task. Although she acknowledges risks that are successful, she has been known to penalize employees when their efforts produce less-than-positive results. This undermines employees' efforts. Innovation stalls and creative risk taking diminishes. Her actions totally destroy trust. Hannah struggles with coaching that attempts to help her see where her actions are contributing to the breakdown of a potentially empowered team.

Because empowerment lives only in a culture of trust, your managerial challenge is to create such an environment. This is where your enlightened power really comes into play. Set the expectations that all employees will do their best possible work, and you model the same. Encourage people to share problems before they ever become nightmares. Allow your power to show up as support for team members and convert any failure into a learning experience. We cannot stress enough that trust is the keystone to empowerment. There is no substitute—and, as you well know, trust can't be faked.

Coaching for You, the Employee

To give your optimal performance on the job, you need to tap into your own *power from within*. We distinguish three areas where empowerment lives: feelings of ownership, accountability, and responsibility. Each one is an attitude you choose that contributes to your sense of being empowered. Ownership comes from the sense that you are a stakeholder and your efforts really make a difference. Accountability makes you answer for your actions. Responsibility moves you to help everyone on the team meet his or her accountabilities.

> *If we did the things we are capable of, we would astound ourselves.*
> —Thomas Edison

Feeling empowered happens best when you fully appreciate the significance and meaning of exactly how your actions contribute to the larger organization. This understanding fuels your inner energy and builds your confidence, all of which translates into performance. You work as part of a community. You connect to the sense of freedom and direction that empowered people enjoy. You honor your employer by accepting the commitments and obligations that the job demands. As an empowered employee, your passion and love for the job are your source of energy. This energy feeds you, guides your approach to different situations, and allows you to share power to get things done. This energy is your internal motivation and compels you to higher levels of performance.

Consider how feeling empowered moved one employee to take new actions. Anna loved the challenge of her new assignment as assistant director of the learning center. She was excited by her manager's invitation to "make a difference" and "be a part of the team." In no time at all, Anna was bursting with ideas about how to streamline various processes for more efficient service to clients. She had one particularly thorny issue in mind that clearly needed attention. Wanting support from everyone, she effectively found a way to present her ideas without challenging or assigning blame to anyone. She used her vision to enlist everyone's support for her plan. Her manager was impressed not only with the level of detail and consideration of the plan but also that Anna had taken on a challenging issue right from the start. Within a month of implementation, operations were running more smoothly. Any mistakes that Anna made were greeted with comments like "I will do better" and "Now I know!" Anna's attitude and energy proved highly contagious to other team members, who started thinking through issues and applying strategies to their own departments.

To be a truly empowered employee, you must see yourself as part of the solution. This means that you assess your own performance and honestly appraise your skills and capabilities. When you encounter problems, you reflect, formulate a strategy, and take decisive action. You find the courage to ask for help when you need it. You use appropriate language to express concerns in positive ways that encourage dialogue. You avoid defensive postures and never speak the language of a victim. You are trustworthy and maintain your real power at all times.

To be an empowered employee requires you to accept accountability for your own career. We want you to find greater meaning and passion in your work. Look for ways that your contributions further the organization. Find every opportunity to add value. Likewise, learn to recognize when your contribution is no longer viable or your interest or passion has moved in another direction. As an empowered employee, recognize when it may be time to change jobs, positions, or even companies (table 7-2).

Table 7-2. Empowerment

What Managers Must Do:	What Employees Must Do:
Create the environment	Self-assess
Foster positive relationships	Become trustworthy
Practice integrity and trust	Accept accountability
Value contributions	Provide solutions
Communicate effectively	Utilize empowering language

The Bottom Line: Harnessing Enlightened Power

Power is the ability to do, act, or strongly and forcibly make an impact. Enlightened power challenges you to discover a new dimension of your real power, using it with savvy to take the right actions for positive results. Real power is another one of those internal elements, much like motivation, attitude, and integrity. It is a state of mind that flows from within and lets you make choices that are rooted in your own truth and strength of character. Real power is something that you uphold and also allow others to uphold. The enlightened power discussed here is deeply connected to your story, which drives your performance.

Enlightened power keeps you informed. You learn to recognize "power tripping" and negative applications of power from positions of authority. You know them for what they are: an attempt to control or coerce. Almost anyone can force another to do things under threat. If your real power has evolved, the effects of negative power will have little influence on you. You are not manipulated or dazzled by some show of force. There is always respect for the positions of leadership and authority, but you never confuse them with real power. You know that influence and an individual sense of shared power are what really shapes direction to produce the right results.

In harnessing your real power to manage others, you become centered in your thoughts and feelings about power and relationships. You transcend being "in charge" as the positional manager, and you encourage actions that both engage and build commitment. Growing into a savvy manager asks you to master that puzzling concept of empowerment, finding a place where you can confidently let go and delegate so your employees can take charge and grow in the process. This is a scary place for many managers, because it is rooted in trust and means surrendering authority. The hardest concept to fully appreciate is that when done well, there is no surrender. Sharing power, empowering others, is something that you are able to do when you are in trusting relationships with your colleagues and your real power has evolved to its highest level.

Use It or Lose It

Write down the one key idea that you "got" as a takeaway from your reading. Then write down what you plan to do starting tomorrow to integrate this idea, practice it, and make it a habit.

1. What I got. _____

_____

2. How I will use it tomorrow. _____

_____

3. Which savvy skill(s) I am developing. _____

_____

Refection Interval

As you begin to build your own confidence and take conscious action to work from your real power, use the story that follows to isolate the characters that live within you. Your choice about who you become is closely aligned to how you choose to act.

The Eagle and the Wolf
Author unknown

There is a great battle that rages inside me. One side is the soaring eagle. Everything the eagle stands for is good and true and beautiful, and it soars above the clouds. Even though it dips down into the valleys, it lays its eggs on the mountaintops.

The other side of me is the howling wolf. And that raging, howling wolf represents the worst that is in me. He eats upon my downfall and justifies himself by his presence in the pack.

Who wins this great battle?

The one I feed.

Coaching for Action: Driving Optimal Performance
Assessing Your Real Power

Take a moment to assess yourself and your personal power. First, think about a time when you felt powerful, effective, successful, and in control:

1. Isolate some of the skills from table 7-1 that showed up for you. *Did you speak your truth? How and for what did you hold yourself accountable? Were you able to make an effective request?*
2. On a scale of 1 (low) to 10 (high), identify how well you used your real power.
3. Looking back, what one action could you have changed that would have created better results?

Likewise, think of a time when you felt powerless:

1. Identify the elements that were missing from that situation. *What actions could you have taken that might have produced a better outcome for you?*
2. Focus on one element from table 7-1. Develop a strategy to make this process skill a stronger force in your power equation.
3. Record your observations and reflections in your journal. Work hard to implement your strategy and strengthen this skill. Notice your results, and shift your actions as you find necessary.

Empowering Your Staff

Develop a plan of action to help your employees become more empowered in the workplace:

1. Choose three of your employees and ask them if they would like help taking a more empowered role at their work.
2. Collaborate to identify areas where each one wants assistance and plan a course of action for each one.
3. Set regular follow-up meetings to help them assess how they are doing and what areas are troubling them.
4. Allow them to take the lead during the feedback sessions.

Lagniappe

Power can truly be your ally in growing yourself and in better managing your team. Learning Annex 7 at www.astd.org/SavvyManager identifies different types of power. Use this discussion to further expand your basic knowledge and apply power judiciously in your workplace.

Developing Authentic Leadership

The art of leadership is liberating people to do what is required of them in the most effective and humane way possible.

—Max DePree

Build your savvy as you learn to

- define authentic leadership
- implement five key qualities required of authentic leaders
- align choices with your values and goals
- distinguish between behaviors of authentic leaders and "wimpy leaders"

The demand for true leadership abounds in all spheres of society today: business, politics, religion, education, communities, and families. Although history is full of people labeled "leader" who clearly possessed the essential attributes and character required to inspire people to excellence, it is also filled with people who garnered their leadership position through force. In and of itself, leadership is a study of both the noble and selfless (Mother Teresa, Gandhi, Martin Luther King Jr.) and the evil and despotic, who coerced people to follow under duress (Hitler, Saddam Hussein). The goal of this chapter is to initiate and ground a more sustainable understanding of leadership that exemplifies more than power over people and manipulation of the external environment.

■ ■ ■

Real Time: Kendall's Story

I can hardly believe that I am getting promoted to general manager of my own facility. This is a new territory, and they have chosen me as the person to create our reputation and grow our business there. I've worked hard for over 10 years, driven by a strong desire to both grow as a manager and add value to the company. It's been a journey up through the ranks, always looking for new opportunities to lead. I've thrived with good managers and survived with some really awful ones. Funny, I learned a lot from both.

I know exactly what I want to create: an environment focused on our clients. I want five strong capable department heads, people who are fully engaged, eager, and supportive, and who want to grow themselves and our new region. We'll need to be comfortable with one another, to challenge each other, and stand united with the decisions we make. I want this leadership team to think of themselves as a board of directors. In fact, considering the power of words, I think I will name them "the Leadership Board."

I am not blind to the problems my promotion will cause. I know I was selected over several guys who have been with the company longer and appeared to be shoe-ins. Some of them have been acting like they already had the job. One in particular has been making promises about new positions and promotions to other people. Won't they be surprised when the announcement is made. Surprised yes, and very angry too. I'll need a solid strategy to turn any negative energy to my advantage. I've got to harness their talents and diffuse any negative feelings. Unchecked, this could sabotage our success.

So many ideas are running through my mind. I have two days to put together my plan of action before the formal announcement. My opening interview question for my inside people offers them a chance to dream big: "If you could do anything, what would you wish to do differently at the new facility to create our reputation in this market?" For now, I need to stay calm and get centered for what's to follow. I can see my vision. I know what I want to create here. How do I become the leader I really want to be?

■ ■ ■

Your development into an authentic leader, something that is more than good, solid management, is the whole focus of your coaching in this chapter. Competent management delivers a sufficient return-on-investment, consistently high productivity, and efficiencies throughout the workplace. Authentic leadership creates and drives a vision of what's possible. The now-familiar phrase coined by Peter Drucker—"Management is doing things right; leadership is doing the right things"—differentiates management from leadership. Doing the right things requires vision, the ability to make difficult decisions, and genuine insight about yourself.

Authentic leadership is not a contract but a covenant. You see, it isn't you who calls you the leader but the people who freely choose to follow you. It is through their eyes, minds, and hearts that your role as a leader is determined. This is the premise that directs our study of leadership, and we make two critical distinctions. First, our coaching about leadership is about you, the *person*, not any titled position. Opportunities to lead exist throughout all levels of every organization. As you expand your own interpretation of leadership, you will begin to see countless opportunities to practice leadership.

> *Effective leaders put words to the formless longings and deeply felt needs of others.*
>
> —Warren Bennis

Second, you will be examining our interpretation of leadership founded on the core attributes that we believe distinguish a leader. It is from these core principles that leaders find the confidence to act. As you consider our list of core qualities of an authentic leader, look to add your own qualities to the list. Keep in mind that these qualities are fundamental. They absolutely, positively have to be present and developed before any other skills can be effectively utilized.

The savvy skill of evolving takes center stage in our discussion of leadership. It is here that you face a significant hurdle. Becoming an authentic leader, worthy of followers, asks you to examine yourself in relation to the core principles and traits that are unique to leadership. It requires wisdom and courage to move beyond controlling habits and refrain from using manipulative behaviors that force others to do what you want. Authentic leadership becomes an expression of your most intimate being of *what you do*; connecting to deep, core values that represent *who you are*. It means that you refine your self-management and collaboration skills and further develop very distinct leadership competencies. You evolve to always acting consciously, not merely to win the charisma contest but because it is the right thing to do. We want you to become that person who attracts the best people, those who deliberately and purposefully elect to follow you. This shapes you into becoming what Goleman, Boyatzis, and McKee (2002) call a resonant leader.

> *Leadership is not a formula or a program; it is a human activity that comes from the heart and considers the hearts of others. . . .*
> *More than anything else today, followers believe they are part of a system, a process that lacks heart. If there is one thing a leader can do to connect with followers at a human, or better still a spiritual level, it is to become engaged with them fully, to share experiences and emotions, and to set aside the processes of leadership we have learned by rote.*
>
> —Lance Secretan

Leadership at Your Core

All of the literature and theories on leadership give long lists of the skills and competencies unique to leading. Before we talk about skills that allow you to lead, we first address qualities that emanate from within your core and confirm who you are. We have identified five key qualities that we believe are crucial to transitioning into an authentic leader:

- trustworthiness
- moral compass
- caring service
- courage
- wisdom.

These five qualities are a gauge by which to measure yourself, as well as a guideline for judging the leadership performance of those around you. Leadership begins with leading oneself, and therefore these five qualities guide you each day in the workplace as you lead and manage. As you read the descriptions of each quality, consider these questions: *How do these qualities align themselves in your life? In others you choose to follow? In the culture of your organization?*

At the center of authentic leadership lies trust, a principle rooted in the emotional domain of all relationships. Trust links to your integrity; the alignment of what you think, what you say, and what you do. *Trustworthiness* clearly manifests as being honest and sincere in keeping promises. Leaders who are trustworthy do not lie, cheat, or steal. They are reliable and competent and uphold their beliefs, even when it is a very difficult choice to do so. Trustworthiness says that your followers willingly accept your power, authority, and leadership of them, and that you are truly deserving of that honor.

The compass is a simple instrument. It reads the magnetic forces of the Earth and points to magnetic north. An authentic leader has an internal *moral compass* that always points in the right direction. Embedded in the higher commandment of "Do no harm," the moral compass makes clear distinctions between good and bad, right and wrong. For the authentic leader, there is no equivocation about this fact.

The moral compass of the authentic leader points to the greater, common good at the heart of every situation. Authentic leaders believe in the inherent value that everyone brings to the organization. This helps to further define the leadership quality of *caring service*. Authentic leaders find value in the service they both give and receive from others. It is in the act of serving others that their leadership exists, not in the expression of their own ego. Caring service, like trust, flows from meaningful relationships. It comes from the heart.

> *Work is a game of the heart as well as the mind.*
> —Lance Secretan

Authentic leaders are the personification of *courage*. Courage is required in choosing actions that support the vision of your organization, especially when an easier target is evident. It is present in every conversation that extends beyond quick decisions. It is harnessed in truly knowing and believing in yourself and others and manifesting those beliefs at a core level. Courage is indispensable in holding to your beliefs about what is possible for your organization, your community, and yourself.

Wisdom is also a quality of the authentic leader. Wisdom blends intelligence, knowledge, and learning with street smarts. It is born of your experiences and your reflections. This reflection informs your actions, which evolve from deeper insights, and furthers your intellectual versatility and discernment. Wisdom expands your capacity to realize what is of value in life for both yourself and others.

Let's examine how these five qualities of leaders show up in the workplace. Consider this scenario. You attend the company's annual strategic planning session, where organizational goals for the coming year are formulated. Upon returning to your office, you call your team together and share these company goals with them. Along with that, you assign components of the larger goal to every person within your department. Each employee is given quantifiable numbers and target objectives, measurable in quarterly increments, for the new fiscal year. As the department manager, you created the plan and shared it down the line. *Does this sound familiar?*

Now consider a different scenario that exemplifies authentic leadership. You call your team together, share the information, and then ask questions. You might inquire, *How might each of you use your talents and gifts to help our department achieve these goals?* Or you might ask, *In what way would each of you like to contribute toward accomplishing these goals?* Your team will be watching and judging what you do next. You employ your savvy skill of self-management and you are quiet, controlling both your emotions and body language. Connecting to your inner wisdom, you allow what is going to happen to manifest, in its own natural way and time.

> *Courage is not simply one of the virtues but the form of every virtue at the testing point.*
> —C. S. Lewis

It takes courage to be silent, to not leap in and hand out job assignments and quotas. You must trust and believe in your employees. Your moral compass must be set to the place where you truly see your employees as people with gifts. Because employees are more accustomed to having goals assigned to them, it will take time for the reality that you've given them a choice to seep into their consciousness. With wisdom, you recognize that each person has something of value that he or she can contribute to the organization's success. It takes caring to honor that value and foster its emergence.

Model a way of being a leader that offers opportunities to serve. Manage any fears or doubts. Your employees will rise to the challenge to help achieve the organization's goals. They want to contribute. Because you have made requests for participation and not given assignments and orders, it may take a day or two for team members to reflect on exactly how they want to contribute. You must allow them the space to find their voices and discern how they will serve.

Choose your next steps from several options. Give your team time to think and reflect, and set another group meeting in a few days. Set individual meetings to explore the possibilities for contributions for each person privately. Follow the private meeting with team meetings and a little fanfare. Invest the time and effort in making leadership choices a part of your routine. And remember that change takes time. Whatever you decide, make it an authentic action.

As you can see, leadership is about observing situations, consciously showing up in a certain manner, and deliberately acting to encourage and engage. It is all about who you are and how you inspire others to become their best. Leadership is about the millions of little, often unnoticed things that you do to better the work environment. The strategies and questions offered in table 8-1 will help you uncover your current approach to each of the five key leadership qualities. Your answers will show you ways to enhance what you are currently doing to lead with savvy.

 Savvy Translation: Savvy managers lead from the core. They leverage the five principles of leadership to guide both their own performance and that of their followers.

Table 8-1. Building Your Leadership Qualities

Quality	Savvy Strategies, Questions, and Behaviors
Trustworthiness	Check your own integrity quotient. Are your actions always aligned with your words? Begin today to practice one of two choices: speaking the truth or being silent. Make a concerted effort to become someone worthy of the trust of others.
Moral Compass	Identify the source of your moral and ethical beliefs. Do these come from the teachings of the Judeo-Christian tradition? What do they support? Whom do they serve? Take aligned actions that fully honor your moral compass.
Caring Service	Strengthen your own confidence so that your needs for glory are about your team, not yourself. What are you doing to help others achieve their goals? Think of yourself as one *with* others, rather than one *over* others.
Courage	Identify the blocks to your leadership. Do you have the courage to face your fears and challenge the status quo? Find your strength to make the tough calls, quickly and decisively. What will you do to hold on to your vision of what's possible? How will you share that vision with your followers?
Wisdom	Access your wisdom through stillness and introspection to clearly see beyond what initially shows up. Can you step back and decipher the underlying elements of what's happening? Are you growing your wisdom with new learning and experiences?

The Light and the Shadow

Next, we want to explore the crucial dialectic of *light and shadow* that exists within the domain of leadership. This connects directly to the leadership qualities described above. Because leaders show up like both Mother Teresa and Hitler, it becomes essential for you to discern the intentions and motivation of the leader. You must learn to recognize how leadership, your own and that of others, engages the actions of followers. Two critical dimensions identify which side of the leadership dialectic is working: the actions/behaviors being demonstrated, and the person taking the actions.

The light side of leadership is all about influence and relationships. It is where a sense of belonging and participation are created, and where acknowledgment of contribution thrives. This leadership requires a higher degree of personal insight into what is really important—what truly inspires people to contribute

> *Leadership is the capacity and will to rally men and women to a common purpose and the character which inspires confidence.*
>
> —Bernard Montgomery

their best, to continually maximize their full potential. Leadership and followership are centered on a vision in which people freely choose to align and engage their actions. From the light side of leadership, performance and behaviors supporting leadership are distinguished, encouraged, and reinforced. Care is taken in making decisions that will have an impact on those employees who are the least able to absorb unpleasant outcomes. All employees are apprenticed to take responsibility, to be accountable for their actions, and to participate in a climate open to growth and opportunity.

The shadow side of leadership is seductive. It places personal gain, along with power and control, above everything and everyone. It induces people to relinquish core values and beliefs for short-term gain. It lulls people into complacency where they can more easily be manipulated or exploited, two practices that constitute true nonleadership. The shadow side of leadership sells others on behaviors often linked to incentives and rewards, taking advantage of people's inherent needs and desires. Paternalistic and benevolent shadow leaders promise security and safety. The recent corporate scandals—like Enron, WorldCom, Arthur Andersen, Adelphia, Global Crossings, and Tyco—give witness to the shadow side of leadership and its tragic results.

Employees accept the shadow side of leadership when they are rewarded materialistically, accepting payment for doing as they are told. They become trapped victims of a system that can easily exploit them. They lose courage and stop questioning orders that fall outside their ethical boundaries. Their moral compasses quit working. Needs get replaced with greed, which easily supports this dark side of leadership.

When you begin to expose this light-and-shadow dialectic, authentic leadership becomes illuminated. Actions that reflect an integrated understanding of the values, goals, and interests of both the individual and the larger community become choices that you make. Realizing these interdependencies makes you adept in developing your own authenticity as a leader.

 Savvy Translation: Savvy managers know that the light side of leadership produces sustainable results for everyone, at a level that can never be attained from the shadow side of leadership.

Leader Descriptors

With an understanding of the light and shadow sides of leadership and a clear picture of the core qualities inherent in authentic leadership, we ask you to consider your personal strengths in relation to five attributes of leadership, which are given in table 8-2. We believe that these practices are embraced and modeled by every great leader. At first glance, you may assess these as very simplistic and obvious. However,

Table 8-2. Leader Descriptors

Descriptor	Explanation	Savvy Translation
Leaders are comfortable in their own skin.	When the elements of emotional intelligence and relationship management coalesce, you become comfortable with who you are. Your pretenses vanish. As you strengthen your own character, you act more authentically and your confidence in your own capabilities expands. You are more open to others and to new possibilities that were invisible before.	Savvy managers don't "do" leadership. By virtue of their character, they are people who live leadership and are therefore worthy to follow.
Leaders offer an inspiring vision.	Authentic leaders share a vision that attracts and inspires others who choose to make it a reality. Inspired visions enroll others and clearly guide all actions and choices.	Savvy managers touch the universal vision that is deeply felt and often unexpressed by others. People want to be part of something bigger than themselves.
Leaders bring out the best in others.	Authentic leaders grow people! They focus their energies on others, nurturing talent and providing specific feedback directed toward personal development and learning. Because a leader's drive and motivation come from an intrinsic level, the focus is on helping people hone their skills and perform to full potential.	Savvy managers live with a worldview of service. They are shepherds, servants to others, encouraging talents that are pooled to produce outstanding results for everyone.
Leaders move seamlessly between the roles of leader and follower.	Shifting between leader and follower becomes a natural flow and ebb predicated on the needs of the moment. The concerns for title give way to a larger desire to foster the vision, collaborate efforts, and empower the actions of others.	Savvy managers are exceptional followers. They understand that the relationship is dynamic. They recognize that even as followers, they are also serving as leaders.
Leaders are resilient.	More than tenacity and perseverance, resilience lets you move conscientiously through challenges. Resilience helps sustain your vision through doubts and fears. It lets you continue on your chosen course in spite of threats and tough decisions.	Savvy managers have an unfailing ability to respond positively and appropriately to whatever occurs. They see obstacles and setbacks as opportunities that help them refine their wisdom. This then energizes them and informs their future actions.

taking action from who you are *being* and how you are showing up for others on a consistent basis is hard work. Don't believe us? Try it! Choose one of the five attributes and fully focus on incorporating it into how you show up for the next day or two. Notice what is revealed.

> *The challenge of leadership is to be strong but not rude; to be kind but not weak; to be bold but not a bully; to be thoughtful but not lazy; to be humble but not timid; to be proud but not arrogant; to have humor but without folly.*
>
> —Jim Rohn

As you review table 8-2, reflect on how well you are manifesting each of these leadership attributes. Focus on new ways in which you can internalize them into your life. Take the time to deeply reflect on the savvy translation that accompanies each descriptor. Grow your savvy as you make each of these a real part of your leadership role.

The Bottom Line: Developing Authentic Leadership

Leadership is that elusive concept—constantly discussed and studied as the foundation of every successful organization. So many authors have written about leadership and the place from which it flourishes. Our concentration on authentic leadership has been rooted in foundational principles that shape your thinking and thus direct your behaviors and actions.

We have coached you to discover your own core qualities, and we conclude with three very specific behaviors that we use to distinguish leadership. First, leaders have a compelling vision that initially functions as a magnet. This is what attracts people to a leader and to the picture or story of what they too can be as a leader. Because you act from core principles, others recognize your vision as one worthy of achieving. As a manager and leader, you continually check that vision and work to keep it strongly planted in the minds and hearts of all your employees. As you continue to live and model your vision, it becomes the glue that holds everyone together.

Second, authentic leaders take decisive action. Acting consciously, they make decisions that give meaning, engage people, and align performances that drive results that are in tandem with company profits. Their actions are chosen not because they will be popular or look good to others but because they are the right choices—always. The essential leadership qualities of caring service and a solid moral compass are rooted in decisive action. Indecisiveness and uncertainty are replaced with confidence, clarity of purpose, and courage.

Third, leaders honestly know themselves. They have a true sense of self and a high degree of personal insight into what is really important. They work from the light side of leadership to capture the hearts, minds, and spirits of people who willingly choose to follow them. They excel in the art of relationship building, creating synergies and harmony among groups that shape organizational culture as a place where leadership resides. Their authenticity is magnetic.

While we coach you on actions we want you to take, and continue to highlight the positive side of situations, we found something a little different to share. It identifies several behaviors of a "wimpy" leader. Read and reflect to uncover if any of these actions are part of your leadership formula.

You are a wimpy leader if. . .

- ◼ Your greatest business goal is to stay within the budget.
- ◼ You are preoccupied with being liked (or not disliked).
- ◼ You reduce goals and performance standards because you think your staff can't meet them.
- ◼ You have been known to say, "We tried that and it doesn't work."
- ◼ When contemplating new ventures, you emphasize the dangers of failure instead of the potential for success.
- ◼ Your decisions are safe and not particularly innovative.

(Reprinted with permission from *Leadership Breakthrough One Handbook*, Rapport Leadership International, 2006.)

Use It or Lose It

Write down the one key idea that you "got" as a takeaway from your reading. Then write down what you plan to do starting tomorrow to integrate this idea, practice it, and make it a habit.

1. What I got. _____

   _____

2. How I will use it tomorrow. _____

   _____

3. Which savvy skill(s) I am developing. _____

   _____

Reflection Interval

The story below offers a unique perspective on leadership. As you read it, think about how the actions of the two different leaders produce results. Are your actions like one of the shepherds? Are you getting the results you want for your team?

The Shepherds

By Joe Batten—reprinted with permission

In the Middle East, there are two countries separated only by a border, with large sheep and mutton industries. The cultures of the two countries are radically different and hostile to each other. In one country, the shepherds walk behind their flocks. In the other, the shepherds walk in front of their flocks.

In the country where the shepherds always walk behind their flocks, the quality of the mutton and the wool is poor, and it is not a profitable industry. In the country where the shepherds walk in front of their flocks, the quality of the mutton and the wool is excellent and the profit is high. Why?

In the country where the shepherd walks behind and pushes, drives, corrects, and is always in charge, the young sheep grow up afraid to stray from the flock for fear of being tapped on the head by the shepherd's staff. They have no opportunity to explore for better grass and water or to play with other young lambs. They simply become obedient, passive, apathetic, and unhealthy.

In the country where the shepherds walk in front of their flocks, the young lambs have plenty of opportunity to stray, play, experiment, and then catch up to the flock. Instead of feeling overcontrolled and compressed, repressed, depressed, and suppressed, they feel free, empowered, enhanced, stretched, and healthy. They eat more, sleep better, and grow up large and healthy. They are truly led.

Coaching for Action: Driving Optimal Performance
Role Models Show the Way

Role models are people who are where you want to be. These people exhibit the skills and talents that you want to emulate.

1. Make a list of five people (living or dead) who you believe to be exceptional leaders; people who you would follow without question; people who exemplify the qualities that you want to develop.
2. Now, holding these people in your mind, develop a list of 10 qualities that are the essence of what makes these people leaders in your eyes.
3. Choose one quality and spend the next month fully developing it for yourself in every thought, word, and deed. Then choose another quality and repeat the process.

Putting Principles into Practice

Operationalizing the qualities and characteristics that we contend are germane to authentic leadership requires reflection. Table 8-3 utilizes the L-E-B model (chapter 1), and speech acts (chapter 6). It presents an integrated perspective of an evolving, authentic leader. From the observer that you are (chapter 2), assess your leadership:

1. Study the qualities and how they emerge in the language, emotions, and body awareness.
2. What shows up for you as strong, positive leadership from the list?
3. What are the areas that require more development or improvement?
4. Choose one area to work on and prepare a written development plan of what you intend to do this next week to incorporate this attribute into your natural way of being.

Table 8-3. Leadership Guide to Language, Emotions, and Body Awareness

Quality	Language	Emotion	Body/Somatic Awareness
Trustworthiness	• Speak the truth. • Keep your commitments and promises. • Really listen, hearing the meaning behind the words.	• Feel an honest connection with followers as equals having different responsibilities. • Feel honor and respect for those you lead.	• Look yourself in the mirror. • Make eye contact with others.
Moral Compass	• Integrity directs your thoughts and actions.	• Choose the light over shadow. • Experience love, concern, and joy in leading.	• You are stable and grounded. • Stand tall for what you know is right.
Caring Service	• Speak using "we" and "us." • Clearly articulate expectations. • Extend opportunities to accept responsibility and grow on the job.	• Feel compelled to bring out the best in others. • Create contagious passion, enthusiasm, and excitement.	• Appropriately show affection to others. • Expand the space for inclusiveness.
Courage	• Inspire with your compelling vision. • Reveal both the good and bad possibilities.	• Recognize and manage your own fears. • Handle the stress of making difficult decisions.	• Move with purpose. • Serve as a magnet for others who follow.
Wisdom	• Choose simple words and common expressions. • Invite others to contribute their ideas, talents, thoughts. • Use appropriate words for saying the right thing.	• Feel confident and believe in yourself and others. • Show calmness to steady others. • Feel worthy and at peace.	• Be comfortable with who you are. • Embody dignity, grace, and self-worth in all actions.

Lagniappe

Leadership, with all its perspectives, is necessary for every company to be successful. Your lagniappe here offers insights into the foundations of leadership and theories that have been used to define it. Expand your learning and visit the Learning Annexes 6 and 8 on www.astd.org/SavvyManager.

Living Your Learning

You are the first organization you must master.
—Stuart Heller

Build your savvy as you learn to

- define embodied learning as a tool to enhance performance
- develop four competencies that grow your capacity to learn
- position yourself as a lifelong learner

What does learning have to do with being a manager? The answer to this question is tied to the expression "If the only tool you have is a hammer, then everything must be a nail!" Clearly, every manager needs more than just a "hammer" in his or her toolbox! Our intent is to expand your tool kit, to provide you with a plethora of tools for managing better. What we know is that each of us succeeds to that place where we have developed our potential for success. If we want to go higher, we must become avid learners. As coaches, we advocate learning as a one of the most powerful tools for advancing your career and helping you and your team reach new levels of performance.

We define learning as new understanding occurring at a higher level of consciousness during your everyday work challenges. Conscious learning is a holistic practice that informs the actions you take. It extends beyond memorizing data or facts. When you are truly learning, you are able to consistently apply conscious actions to produce the results you want. To reach this level of conscious learning requires you to utilize all the savvy managerial skills.

■ ■ ■

Real Time: Johnnie's Story

The lyrics to that song keep playing in my head. You know that oldie about getting out of this place—that there's something better out there. I've been stuck here for too long. I know it's past time for me to do something. That's why I'm here at this workshop. Hopefully, it will reenergize me, really move me to another place!

I admit that I've been obsessive about controlling everything. I made myself indispensable and irreplaceable, stifling not only my own career but also that of my key people. Sue's promotion last month was my reality check. That position should have been mine! But based on what my district manager observed, Henry didn't think any of my staff was ready to take over my job. If I had to do it all, then they must not be capable! Talk about sabotaging your own career!

On the bright side, I proudly claim some department successes. The coaching I've done for the past two years is paying off. Jim still occasionally hesitates over decisions, running things by me first, but his team's numbers look great and his people seem happy! Melanie is finding her groove. Her questions and suggestions during our meetings show she's getting it. She misses some of her targets, but she's quick to rebound and always considers her missteps as learning opportunities, not failures. She has a great attitude! Wish I could bottle it!

My friend Phil came to this workshop last year. He is a changed man with renewed energy, a new focus. Phil even made salesman of the year! I want those same results. The more I think about it, the more I realize that I can never lose focus about my own personal professional development. And, as the manager, I must help each of my employees grow and develop, too! It's the only way we will all get ahead.

Here he comes. We're starting. I know I am at a turning point in my career. Whoa, I need to figure out what I need to learn. What will take me to that next level? I am so ready! I hope this guy works the same magic on me as he did for Phil!

■ ■ ■

Learning promotes thinking differently. You self-manage and don't jump to conclusions. You allow the meaning of events to more fully reveal themselves. Subtle connections emerge as you reflect on what is happening. Deeper insights and understanding produce more conscious actions. Sharper focus enables more effective execution. We are coaching you to recognize the power of learning as a means of collaborating—of integrating the autonomous, yet interconnected, work from all your highly skilled people. Learning, an *equal-opportunity proficiency*, can become your ultimate strategic business tool.

Intentional learning takes time to develop and to become part of your conscious activity. When learning, or any practice, embeds itself at the deeper level described here, it is considered embodied. You might know this concept by its other name, habit. Embodied learning, like sustainable change, is the ultimate goal. It helps you rethink critical processes and behaviors in the dynamic context of business today. Figure 9-1 shows the evolutionary process of learning. Spiraling into ever-increasing levels of effectiveness as new learning takes hold, organizations reap the ultimate

Figure 9-1. The Learning Spiral

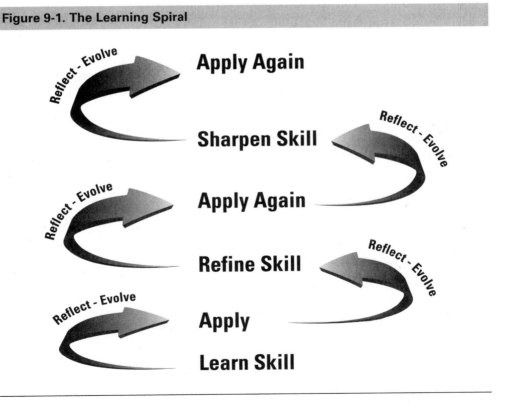

benefit that comes from acquired skills and knowledge. The goal of this chapter is to help you discover how to incorporate the practices of learning into your repertoire and use embodied learning to enhance your results.

Embodied Learning

There are three basics types of learning. The first two, informational and skill development, are the most familiar kinds. Informational learning focuses on gathering facts or data. Skill development entails specific learning required to perform a particular task. Our coaching centers on the third type of learning, embodied learning. With embodied learning, you consciously incorporate new information in a way that becomes habit.

> *The closer you get to the heart of yourself, the more you realize that what stops you is not outside you. It is within you.*
>
> —Stuart Heller

By way of an example of embodied learning, think back to the time when you were learning to drive a car—more precisely, learning to drive a standard stick shift. Remember? Clutch, shift into gear, smooth clutch release, with slow acceleration on the gas pedal. When you first began, you had to concentrate on every action, including trying to keep the car in your own lane while you studied your feet! When you got proficient, these actions became automatic, requiring little mental effort. Driving with a standard shift became so routine that if you changed to a vehicle with an automatic transmission, you might occasionally "clutch" the floor. Your learning to drive a stick shift became totally embodied, and you just did it!

Deep-seated, embodied learning produces automatic actions, effectively targeted to respond to current situations. Embodied learning helps you to explore more complex situations with newfound power. The observer who you are assesses what is happening more completely, exposing the various nuances and subtleties. A deeper appreciation for the myriad connections and possibilities emerges. Your options for action expand with each turn around the spiral. You may want to go back and review figure 9-1. New information and skills intertwine, becoming embedded into your core, as your habitual way of being.

Embodied learning produces a change within you, allowing you to take action more quickly. It prepares you to respond naturally in an effective manner, without reactionary behaviors. The distinction here is much the same as *being* a savvy manager rather than *doing* managerial work. With embodied learning, you grow your ability to choose effectively; to build relationships that enable work. When you understand the value that comes from conscious learning, you truly expand yourself. It is very important that you understand this concept. Take your time thinking it through and reflect on the distinction being made here.

The story of Carl, an angry and confused manager, exemplifies the process that occurs with embodied learning. Carl felt overworked and unappreciated. He kept wondering why he was never offered advancement opportunities. He was irritated with what he observed as arbitrary changes in things like vacation policy and project assignments. For

> *Without active learning, all people can expect is a commodity career where they are treated like replaceable merchandise.*
>
> —Calhoun W. Wick
> and Lu Stanton León

months, his anger festered. It was all management's and the company leadership's fault, and Carl's conversations reflected his victim mentality. All three domains—pessimistic language, angry festering emotions, and physical stress—were present and highly active in Carl's life.

To help shift his perspective, Carl's coach suggested that he read a powerful little book, *The Four Agreements*, by Don Miguel Ruiz (1997). The book outlines a simple bargain the reader makes with himself or herself to uphold four principles. Carl read the book and something clicked. Though it is hard to pinpoint the actual learning nugget that Carl received from reading the book, it definitely challenged and upset the coherency of his victim story. As he began to practice the four principles, he began to comprehend—*learn*—that he had more control over what was happening in his life. He took ownership of his choices. He finally realized how his perceptions had created his story and were controlling his actions. With one shift in that connection, a series of new possible actions emerged. Within days, he was thinking about taking additional classes and relocating to pursue new management opportunities. Within seven months, Carl had a whole new life filled with different and exciting challenges. *Learning!*

Embodied learning happens at multiple levels. For Carl, it started as mental learning that touched an emotional chord, all of which then manifested as a physical expression steering him to new, positively directed behaviors. As the domains of language, emotions, and body aligned for Carl, his space for acting consciously enlarged. (See the discussion of the L-E-B Model in chapter 1.) His savvy ability increased.

Think about what aligning your own thoughts, words, and actions could do to drive your own performance. Embodied learning touches you at your very core; it changes the observer who you are at a fundamental place. It lets you finally make sense of your experiences in ways that allow you to truly let go when you need to. You are released from old habits and behaviors that no longer serve you. Learning is an empowering gift you give to yourself. It moves you forward. You become open to continually discovering new realities and producing better results. You evolve!

 Savvy Translation: Savvy managers always embark on a track that generates embodied learning for growing and sustaining changes within their organization. They know that when the learning is not embodied, any effort is temporary.

Stages of the Learning Process

Learning, especially embodied learning, happens over time and in stages that progress from low to high levels of competence. As you and your team work on projects, it is interesting and insightful to discover where you are in the learning process. Each learning stage poses its own set of challenges. Howell's (1982) descriptive terms show how people proceed through different stages of learning, and they still serve as a useful tool to gauge your own progress. The stages are described in table 9-1. As you advance through the stages, your capacity to be effective in all areas of your performance grows, too.

> *Learning [is]... expanding the ability to produce the results we truly want in life.*
>
> —Anonymous

To help you more fully understand each of these stages, we will walk you through a familiar scenario. Because you are technically competent in your position, you have now been promoted into a managerial position. Congratulations! You now begin your process of really learning to become a manager. As you read through each of the learning stages, see table 9-1 to get your savvy translation coaching points.

Howell's first stage of learning, *unconscious incompetence,* is a state of blissful ignorance where your confidence often exceeds your ability. It is the stage in which you are unaware of all that you really need to learn. The joy of promotion, your higher rank and title, and increased salary and benefits all feel so good. You start to believe the false information that management is just common sense. Off you go ready to fix all the people and problems that you thought were wrong when that "other guy" was in charge. Even with some basic planning and problem-solving skills, as a new

Table 9-1. Stages of Learning

Stage	Explanation	Savvy Translation
Unconscious incompetence	You don't know that you don't know.	Realizing that you don't know is the key here. Savvy managers know that not knowing gives an unacceptable advantage to others. The savvy manager doesn't get confounded by ego but actively seeks to uncover his or her blind spots.
Conscious incompetence	You know that you don't know.	Savvy managers most often start here. You know that not knowing can derail results. You use your personal power to direct the learning you need. Savvy managers ask for help!
Conscious competence	You know that you know.	You see your awareness growing, which reinforces your budding assessment of competence. You know that your competence may be fleeting as new changes and innovations occur. You continually monitor your results and make changes as necessary.
Unconscious competence	You really know you know.	Your actions are fluid. You have embodied the process through reflection, observation, perception, and interpretation. You effectively navigate changes that get thrown your way. You are in the zone!
Conscious unconscious competence	You teach, mentor, and continually develop.	You look for every opportunity to coach, mentor, and teach others so that they can work to their full potential. You are striving toward Maslow's highest level of human needs, self-actualization.

Source: Howell (1982); Pike (1994); Maslow (1998).

manager you likely lack the readiness and the insight to effectively manage your employees as the unique individuals they really are. The bottom line is that you don't know that you don't know!

During the second stage, *conscious incompetence*, the honeymoon is over. You begin to discover there are pieces missing and how little you really know about managing. What once seemed like common sense now takes on a whole new dimension. The realities of what it takes to successfully interact with your staff, much less begin to inspire and lead them, appear more elusive and difficult than first thought. Accompanying your discovery of these skill shortcomings are often feelings of discomfort and a diminished sense of confidence. "What have I gotten myself into?" might be the question haunting your dreams. As a new manager, you might retreat into self-protective reactions and avoidance behaviors or try to do it all yourself. Many managers spend their entire careers at this stage, never seeking or even realizing they need help. Others recognize when things are not working. Seeing what works and what doesn't is a true learning experience. When your savvy skills emerge, you begin to seek help in books or courses. You accept assignments at work that challenge and stretch you. You seek out mentors, teachers, and coaches. You know you need to gain competency, so you establish learning as an integral part of your life.

In the third stage of learning, you are becoming *consciously competent*. You are internalizing new information and practicing new managerial skills. Your confidence increases as you recognize your growing abilities to effectively manage. You have awareness about your own actions and how they affect others. You are reflecting on your actions, especially when you become aware that a certain action is not working.

> *We invest so much in what we know that we refuse to give it up, even when it has stopped serving us.*
> —Julio Olalla

You are learning the nuances of people and processes through collaboration and reflection. You recognize the importance of the ebb and flow of relationships. Your performance is growing. Although you still cannot get out of your own way all of the time, you are hitting more home runs and striking out a lot less.

Unconscious competence is the fourth stage of learning. You are now increasingly more comfortable and competent in attaining the results you really want. Your skills and behaviors blend together and become habits as your ability to manage becomes embodied learning. Confidence peaks at this stage as a new dimension of your managerial role emerges. You perform with ease, leading and directing the workflow. Others who depend on you are also increasingly getting the results they want from you. Your enhanced ability to use the tools presented in the previous chapters (the ladder of inference, observer positions, perceptual prisms, mindsets, reflection) has become habitual. Your ability to assimilate and synthesize learning to new situations is high.

The fifth stage of learning, *conscious unconscious competence*, was added to Howell's model by Bob Pike (1994). Pike believed that at this level you transfer what you learn to others almost unknowingly, just from your *being* and living what you have learned. In our example, your modeling of certain abilities attracts people to you. They want to learn from you and you find ways to help others develop their learning capacities. Effortlessly, you become more of a mentor, coaching performances and developing your team. It is the application of the adage that you really know something when you can teach it to another person. In this case, your teaching is a sharing or collaborative approach to managing your people.

All of us move through these five stages of learning throughout our lives as different events and new challenges present themselves. Think back to situations when you were first learning a skill or behavior. At the beginning of any new learning curve, you are unaware of all that you don't know. The more you embody learning as a holistic process, the more aware you become about what you need to fully comprehend. Learning to identify what you don't know is as important as knowing what you do know. The savvy person will always ask that critical question, *In which stage of learning am I for this situation?* Your answer gives you the information you need to move to the next stage.

Into the Learning Zone

Like the competencies and skills explored thus far, learning how to learn happens when you actively choose to integrate and develop your learning capacity. As with most new skills, your actions will take effort and conscious thought, as well as long-term commitment. You will have to pay attention to what you are doing. With each small step, you will feel encouraged to keep trying new and different learning activities. Your payoff is a smarter, more savvy you! This last section identifies skills essential for embodied learning:

- challenging assumptions
- risk taking
- curiosity
- practice.

The habits fostered by these skills will transform you into a lifelong learner. First, your *ability to challenge assumptions* initiates every learning process. It is in the action of challenging your assumptions that your interpretations are clearly revealed. Once exposed, you can reconsider your beliefs within current circumstances to see if those perspectives and assumptions still hold true. If they do, then your actions will reflect that constancy. When they don't hold true, when circumstances have changed, you consciously take new actions.

Your receptivity to consider new information that challenges your beliefs and assumptions, individually and organizationally, is a fundamental step toward embodied learning. Because so much of what you believe to be true is transparent to you, you have already embodied practices. Some still work well, but others no longer serve you effectively. By now, your ability to uncover deeply held assumptions and to clarify them in relation to reality and the choices you make should be crystallizing for you.

Challenging assumptions links to the habit of *risk taking*, the second capability you must develop. Intelligent, calculated risk taking, not daredevil risks, is required here. Exploring options that offer greater possible outcomes requires courage and patience. *What if* discernment triggers interesting conversations without limits and reveals additional choices. Learning at this level breeds innovation. Innovative thinking expands your playing field. Negative results are seen as just another choice to be avoided in the future. When you begin to follow this process, you can claim to be skilled at learning.

> *Ask yourself every day, which customers did I touch today, and what did I learn?*
>
> —Peter Drucker

The third critical skill is *curiosity*. Curiosity is a wholesome desire to be informed, to see the whole picture. It is distinctly different from prying, meddling, or inquisition, all of which have negative connotations. Learning curiosity is positive, producing that genuine desire to know for all the right reasons. It guides you on multiple pathways to get to the root of an issue. The questioning process inherent in being curious frees you from the need to always be right; to immediately know all the answers. It compels you to question the causal relationships between events. It asks questions that lead you to uncover and disclose, wonder and explore. Developing the ability to ask questions comes from knowing that there are no stupid questions and that every inquiry stirs more interest. With questioning, you can further develop your art of listening, one of the most important habits of any manager.

Finally, we come to *practice*. Think about how you get really good at something—or why some things never get mastered. Practice is usually the missing link. Learning does not root itself firmly into your subconscious until you practice new ways of thinking, feeling, and acting. With practice, new actions cease to feel awkward and uncomfortable, gradually allowing you to embrace the newness of change. This is your ability to put it all together and make it all work seamlessly; to have it become embodied within.

 Savvy Translation: Savvy managers want to grow. To sharpen their skills and competencies, they consciously challenge assumptions, take risks, utilize curiosity, and practice new learning.

The Bottom Line: Living Your Learning

Engaging in life successfully is significantly enhanced by your ability to learn at that deep core level defined as embodied learning. It is the primary competency of the 21st century. Although the phrase "lifelong learner" may seem trite, it truly represents the best opportunity to have what you most want. Your quality of life is uniquely tied to your ability to move with circumstances that are often out of your control. As a lifelong learner, you remain open and eager for new information. You adeptly process new knowledge in a cohesive manner and gain the advantage that acting consciously offers. You have the commitment and tenacity to stick with new learning, practicing until it becomes embodied. Lifelong learners evolve!

Organizations are dynamic entities. The most successful companies are those that have built communities of people who learn together and apply that learning to grow themselves and their business. This is your challenge as a developing savvy manager. Find ways to leverage your learning to generate new possibilities for yourself, your team, and the whole company.

Our work as coaches is all about helping people reach their full potential. It is the reason we stress learning as a competency. Complacency is your real enemy. Without learning, you stagnate. Our clients choose coaching as a method for learning. Coaching lets them question the status quo and drive themselves to optimal performance. Without exception, we continue to see that through coaching our clients grow their learning capacity, which enables them to evolve.

Use It or Lose It

Write down the one key idea that you "got" as a takeaway from your reading. Then write down what you plan to do starting tomorrow to integrate this idea, practice it, and make it a habit.

1. What I got. _____

_____

2. How I will use it tomorrow. _____

_____

3. Which savvy skill(s) I am developing. _____

_____

Reflection Interval

As you read the story below, consider the direction that your own learning has taken in your life. What more do you hope to learn? Can you find the joy and challenge of the newness?

Retooling on the Run
By Stuart Heller and David Sheppard Surrenda—reprinted with permission

In a small town, a young piano player had a dream. Considered to be a child prodigy, his goal was to become an internationally renowned pianist. Far surpassing his teachers, he contemplated traveling to New York to fulfill his dream of studying with a master teacher.

Finally, his chance appeared. He was invited to audition with one of the most renowned teachers in the world. Under the master's knowing gaze, he drew forth his best performance. Afterward, he spoke of the dream of becoming a true virtuoso.

The maestro contemplated what he had just heard and said, "The goal that you wish to achieve is possible, but I do not know if you are prepared to do what it will take. Your performance was excellent. However, your method has very severe limits. You have achieved more with it than I would have expected. The real problem is that the method you are using is not the method of a true virtuoso. It cannot take you to the heights you wish to attain. You have already gone far beyond the limits of your current technique. The path to virtuosity begins by returning to the basics of piano technique in order to reconstruct a method that has open-ended potential.

"Traveling the path I see before you is very difficult. Consciously going back to the beginning is more challenging than you imagine. The issue here is more than physical technique alone. You are the real instrument that must be mastered. All of you is presented in how you play. If you are to be a master, you must learn to face your fears and wrestle with your habits. When you are able to do this successfully, you will be ready to reach within yourself to bring forth your genius."

Coaching for Action: Driving Optimal Performance
Learning!

1. Continue to examine the people and events in your work life. Draw a vertical line down the center of a piece of paper. In the left-hand column, make a list of five people you interact with on a regular basis. In the right-hand column, begin to think about what you might learn from each of these people with whom you work.
2. Now repeat the same process, focusing on two or three projects or job assignments. For each project, attempt to figure out what you can learn that will enable you to grow and how you can assimilate your new learning and apply it to other projects.

Learning Makers and Learning Breakers

If you lead a team, manage a department, or own your own business, knowing what enables or diminishes learning for everyone is essential. Use worksheet 9-1 to identify the learning makers and learning breakers that may be present in your organization.

Plan a growth meeting with your team. Make copies of worksheet 9-1. Bring in lunch and have a conversation about how learning enables the company to stay sharp and competitive in changing times. How can you minimize the effect of any learning breakers in your organization?

Worksheet 9-1. Learning Makers/Learning Breakers

	Learning Makers		Learning Breakers
	Learning is voluntary. Mandatory, forced learning rarely sticks.		Being unable to say and accept that you don't know presents a powerful obstacle to learning.
	Let individuals participate and be accountable for the development of their own learning plan.		Lacking patience for the learning process. Many people want clarity and answers immediately.
	Match the perceived needs, career goals, personal aspirations, and interests of the learner with the learning being presented.		Not being able to laugh at yourself. When you take yourself too seriously, you close an emotional doorway that is also an entry point for learning.
	Allow space and time for living with discomforts that new learning brings. Make room for mistakes!		Assessments from your past about your ability to learn may hinder your ability to learn.
	Fit individual learning into company goals.		Being unable to live in the confusion that learning creates is a barrier to learning.
	Mutual trust and honoring differences extend the learning environment.		Not acknowledging the missing pieces in your life is a great inhibitor to learning.
	An air of lightness should accompany learning; it should be fun!		Failure to practice or not take the opportunity to apply learning where it counts.

Source: Adapted from Newfield Network, Inc.

Lagniappe

Developing your skills and competencies is one way to enhance your performance on the job. Look at the "Personal Performance Assessment" tool in Lagniappe 4 on www.astd.org/SavvyManager. Take a moment to reflect and assess how you perform in one specific area. Use this to further your learning to grow new skills to become a savvy manager.

Acknowledgments

Work like this book is rarely the product from one mind or of one soul. Both authors recognize the contributions of their teachers and coaches in the fields of human development, leadership, coaching, and management—men and women like Peter Drucker, Tom Peters, Jim Collins, Warren Bennis, Meg Wheatley, Max DePree, John Whitmore, Julio Olalla, Timothy Gallwey, and Daniel Goleman. Many of the ideas expressed in our book are our interpretations and applications adapted from the works of these and other distinguished people. It has been a challenge for us to discern where our learning from one of these great teachers stopped and the concepts from another began. Specific citation is given where work has been directly utilized. We encourage you to continue your own savvy development by reading the full works of these enlightened thinkers.

We thank Henry Mintzberg and Ken Wilber for permission to use their concepts as a starting point for our discussion of the five mindsets and the quadrants of consciousness, respectively.

The teachings about ontological coaching and methodologies from the Newfield Network, based in Boulder, have greatly influenced this work and are evident in several tables, a figure, and a worksheet. We are grateful for Newfield's permission to use the Newfield Method in these various derivative ways and interpretations. The diagram used in figure 1-1 is directly reprinted with its permission. To find out more about Newfield and the fundamentals of its method, please see its website, www.newfieldnetwork.com.

We extend thanks to our clients, who have allowed us to share in their learning and development into savvy managers.

A big thank-you also goes to the students in Jane Flagello's management classes at DeVry University, who provided feedback on readability and comprehension. Thanks to our colleagues who read and critiqued chapters, most especially Teresa Oliszewicz for her keen insight and broad perspective on management.

To Mark Morrow, at ASTD Press, we are forever grateful for your belief in our work and your support in sharing it with a wider audience. Additional thanks to Alfred Imhoff and to everyone on the ASTD team for sharing their talents and bringing our book to market.

The encouragement and understanding received from our family and friends have been a huge boost to our labor of love in writing this book.

And finally, our love is extended to John Flagello and Greg Dugas for their unfaltering support, patience, and sustaining encouragement.

References and Suggested Reading

Although the authors have not directly quoted from each of the books and articles listed below, each book or article has added to the development of the perspective taken throughout this book. It is important to acknowledge the vast array of ideas, opinions, and research that goes into moving the practice of management to successively higher levels of quality, innovation, and effectiveness.

Andreas, S., and C. Faulkner, eds. 1994. *NLP: The New Technology of Achievement*. New York: William Morrow.

Argyris, C. 1991. Teaching Smart People How to Learn. *Harvard Business Review* 69, no. 3: 99–110.

———. 1993. *Knowledge for Action*. San Francisco: Jossey-Bass.

———.1998. Empowerment: The Emperor's New Clothes. *Harvard Business Review* 76, no. 3: 98–105.

Austin, J. L. 1973. *How to Do Things with Words*, 2nd ed. Cambridge, MA: Harvard University Press.

Bass, B. M. 1990. *Handbook of Leadership: A Survey of Theory and Research*. New York: Free Press.

Bennis, W. 1989a. *On Becoming a Leader*. Reading, MA: Addison-Wesley.

———. 1989b. *Why Leaders Can't Lead: The Unconscious Conspiracy Continues*. San Francisco: Jossey-Bass.

Bennis, W., and B. Nanus. 1985. *Leaders: The Strategies for Taking Charge*. New York: HarperCollins.

Block, P. 2002. *The Answer to How Is Yes: Acting on What Matters*. San Francisco: Berrett-Koehler.

Bolman, L. G., and T. E. Deal. 1997. *Reframing Organizations: Artistry, Choice and Leadership*, 2nd ed. San Francisco: Jossey-Bass.

Bossidy, L., and R. Charan. 2002. *Execution: The Discipline of Getting Things Done*. New York: Crown.

Bryner, A., and D. Markova. 1996. *An Unused Intelligence: Physical Thinking for 21st-Century Leadership*. Berkeley, CA: Conari Press.

Budd, M., and L. Rothstein. 2000. *You Are What You Say: A Harvard Doctor's Six-Step Program for Transforming Stress through the Power of Language.* New York: Crown.

Byham, W. C. 1997. Characteristics of an Empowered Organization. In *The Power of Empowerment: What Experts Say and 16 Actionable Cases,* ed. W. Ginnodo. Arlington Heights, IL: Pride Publications.

Champy, M. 1995. *Reengineering Management: The Mandate for New Leadership.* New York: HarperCollins.

Collins, J. 2002. *Good to Great: Why Some Companies Make the Leap and Others Don't.* New York: HarperCollins.

Covey, S. R. 1989. *The 7 Habits of Highly Effective People.* New York: Simon & Schuster.

———. 2004. *The 8th Habit.* New York: Simon & Schuster.

DePree, M. 1989. *Leadership Is an Art.* New York: Doubleday.

Doran, G. T. 1981. There Is a SMART Way to Write Management Goals and Objectives. *Management Review,* November, 35–36.

Drucker, P. F. 1954. *The Practice of Management.* New York: Harper & Brothers.

———. 1999. *Management Challenges for the 21st Century.* New York: HarperCollins.

———. 2002a. The Discipline of Innovation. *Harvard Business Review* 80, no. 8: 95.

———. 2002b. *Managing in the Next Society.* New York: Truman Tally Books, St. Martin's Press.

Dunham, R. 2003. The Body of Management. In *Being Human at Work,* ed. R. Heckler. Berkeley, CA: North Atlantic Books.

Dyer, W. 1992. *Real Magic: Creating Miracles in Everyday Life.* New York: HarperCollins.

———. 2004. *The Power of Intention: Change the Way You Look at Things and the Things You Look at Will Change.* Carlsbad, CA: Hay House.

Eiseley, L. 1979. *The Star Thrower.* Fort Washington, PA: Harvest Books.

Flores, F., and R. Solomon. 2001. *Building Trust in Business, Politics, Relationships, and Life.* New York: Oxford University Press.

Gallwey, W. Timothy. 2000. *The Inner Game of Work.* New York: Random House.

Gardner, J. W. 1990. *On Leadership.* New York: Free Press.

Gellerman, S. W. 1992. *Motivation in the Real World: The Art of Getting Extra Effort from Everyone—Including Yourself.* New York: Dutton.

Goleman, D. 1998. *Working with Emotional Intelligence.* New York: Bantam Books.

Goleman, D., R. Boyatzis, and A. McKee. 2002. *Primal Leadership.* Boston: Harvard Business School Press.

Goss, T. 1996. *The Last Word on Power: Executive Re-Invention for Leaders Who Must Make the Impossible Happen.* New York: Currency-Doubleday.

Greenleaf, R. 1997. *Servant Leadership: A Journey into the Nature of Legitimate Power and Greatness.* New York: Paulist Press.

Heckler, R. S. 1990. *In Search of the Warrior Spirit: Teaching Awareness Disciplines to the Green Berets.* Berkeley, CA: North Atlantic Books.

———. 1993. *The Anatomy of Change: A Way to Move through Life's Transitions.* Berkeley, CA: North Atlantic Books.

Hock, D. 1999. *Birth of the Chaordic Age*. San Francisco: Berrett-Koehler.

House, R. J. 1977. A 1976 Theory of Charismatic Leadership. In *Leadership: The Cutting Edge*, ed. J. G. Hunt and L. L. Larson. Carbondale: Southern Illinois University Press.

Howell, W. S. 1982. *Empathic Communicator*. Washington, DC: Wadsworth.

Kegan, R. 1994. *In Over Our Heads: The Mental Demands of Modern Life*. Cambridge, MA: Harvard University Press.

King, R. G. 1979. *Fundamentals of Human Communication*. New York: Macmillan.

Knowles, M. S. 1980. *The Modern Practice of Adult Education: Andragogy versus Pedagogy*. New York: Association Press.

Kostenbaum, P. 1991. *Leadership: The Inner Side of Greatness*. San Francisco: Jossey-Bass.

Kotter, J. 1996. *Leading Change*. Boston: Harvard Business School Press.

Kraines, G. A. 2001. *Accountability Leadership*. Franklin Lakes, NJ: Career Press.

Leeds, D. 2000. *Smart Questions*. New York: Berkley Books.

Lawler, E. E., III. 1992. *The Ultimate Advantage: Creating the High Involvement Organization*. San Francisco: Jossey-Bass.

Leonard, G. 1991. *Mastery: The Keys to Success and Long-Term Fulfillment*. New York: Penguin.

Lewin, K. 1951. *Field Theory in Social Sciences: Selected Theoretical Papers*. New York: Harper & Brothers.

Magretta, J. 2002. *What Management Is: How It Works and Why It Is Everyone's Business*. New York: Free Press.

Maslow, A. 1998. *Maslow on Management*. New York: John Wiley & Sons.

Matejka, K., and R. J. Dunsing. 1995. *A Manager's Guide to the Millennium: Today's Strategies for Tomorrow's Success*. New York: American Management Association.

Maturana, H. R., and F. J. Varela. 1998. *The Tree of Knowledge: The Biological Roots of Human Understanding*, rev. ed. Boston: Shambhala.

McNamara, C. 1999. Basics about Employee Motivation (Including Steps You Can Take). Adapted from *Basic Guide to Management, Leadership and Supervision*, www.mapnp.org.

Mintzberg, H., and J. Gosling. 2002. Educating Managers beyond Borders. *Academy of Management Learning and Education* 1, no. 1: 64–76.

———. 2003. The Five Minds of a Manager. *Harvard Business Review* 81: 54–63.

Mohrman, S. A. 1997. Empowerment: There's More To It Than Meets the Eye. In *The Power of Empowerment: What Experts Say and 16 Actionable Cases*, ed. W. Ginnodo. Arlington Heights, IL: Pride Publications.

Nelson, P. 1993. *There's a Hole in My Sidewalk*. Hillsboro, OR: Beyond Words Publishing.

Olalla, J. March 27, 2000. *Proceedings of Newfield Network Coaching for Personal and Professional Mastery Conference*. Alexandria, VA: Newfield Network, Inc.

Peters, T. 1988. *Thriving on Chaos*. New York: Alfred A. Knopf.

———. 2003. *Re-imagine! Business Excellence in a Disruptive Age*. London: Dorling Kindersley.

Pfeffer, J. 1992. *Managing with Power: Politics and Influence in Organizations*. Boston: Harvard Business School Press.

Pike, B. 1994. *Creative Training Techniques Handbook*, rev. ed. Minneapolis: Lakewood.

Porter, M. 1985. *Competitive Advantage: Creating and Sustaining Superior Performance*. New York: Free Press.

Ruiz, D. M. 1997. *The Four Agreements*. San Rafael, CA: Amber-Allen.

Searle, J. R. 1969. *Speech Acts: An Essay in the Philosophy of Language*. Cambridge: Cambridge University Press.

Secretan, L. H. K. 1997. *Reclaiming Higher Ground: Creating Organizations That Inspire the Soul*. Boston: McGraw-Hill.

———. 2004. *Inspire: What Great Leaders Do*. Hoboken, NJ: John Wiley & Sons.

———. 2006. *One: The Art and Practice of Conscious Leadership*. Caledon, Canada: Secretan Center.

Senge, P. 1990. *The Fifth Discipline: The Art and Practice of the Learning Organization*. New York: Doubleday.

———. 1999. *The Dance of Change*. New York: Doubleday.

Senge P., C. Roberts, R. B. Ross, B. J. Smith, and A. Kleiner. 1994. *The Fifth Discipline Fieldbook: Strategies and Tools for Building a Learning Organization*. New York: Currency Books.

Shechtman, M. R. 1994. *Working without a Net: How to Survive and Thrive in Today's High-Risk Business World*. Englewood Cliffs, NJ: Prentice Hall.

Sieler, A. 2003. *Coaching to the Human Soul: Ontological Coaching and Deep Change*. Blackburn, Australia: Newfield Australia.

Smith, R. M. 1982. *Learning How to Learn: Applied Theory for Adults*. Englewood Cliffs, NJ: Cambridge Adult Education.

Somers, K. 1997. Defining the Boundaries of Empowerment. In *The Power of Empowerment: What Experts Say and 16 Actionable Cases*, ed. W. Ginnodo. Arlington Heights, IL: Pride Publications.

Steers, R. M., L. W. Porter, and G. A. Bigley. 1996. *Motivation and Leadership at Work*. New York: McGraw-Hill.

Von Ghyczy, T., B. Von Oetinger, and C. Bassford, eds. 2001. *Clausewitz on Strategy: Inspiration and Insight from a Master Strategist*. New York: John Wiley & Sons.

Weisinger, H. 1998. *Emotional Intelligence at Work*. San Francisco: Jossey-Bass.

Wheatley, M. 1992. *Leadership and the New Science*. San Francisco: Berrett-Koehler.

———. 2002. *Turning to One Another: Simple Conversations to Restore Hope to the Future*. San Francisco: Berrett-Koehler.

Whitmore, J. 1998. *Coaching for Performance*. London: Nicholas Brealey.

Wick, C. W., and L .L. Stanton León. 1993. *The Learning Edge: How Smart Managers and Smart Companies Stay Ahead*. New York: McGraw-Hill.

Wilber, K. 1996. *A Brief History of Everything*. Boston: Shambhala.

Winograd, T., and F. Flores. 1986. *Understanding Computers and Cognition: A New Foundation for Design*. Norwood, NJ: Ablex.

About the Authors

Jane R. Flagello, EdD, is an enthusiastic, results-oriented professional with more than 30 years of experience in business and education. She believes that organizations bring about sustainable change and become great places to work when employees learn new ways of interacting with one another. Her coaching focuses on the core domains of communication, team effectiveness, leadership development, conflict resolution, and career management. She has worked with organizations in manufacturing, education, and technology and has assisted entrepreneurs with business startups. She is a senior professor at DeVry University's Addison, Illinois, campus, where her application-oriented teaching style bridges the theory-to-practice gap. Her doctorate is in adult continuing education from Northern Illinois University. She is a certified ontological coach and a certified client facilitator of the Covey 7 Habits of Highly Effective People program.

Sandra Bernard Dugas, PhD, is a professional executive coach, master trainer, and facilitator. Her successful Lafayette, Louisiana, businesses have garnered national recognition. She serves as an adjunct faculty member of the Human Capital Development PhD Program and the Master of Science in Workforce Training and Development Graduate Program at the University of Southern Mississippi. She also serves as a facilitator in the Training and Development Certificate Program at the Jack and Patti Phillips Workplace Learning and Performance Institute. Through her coaching/facilitating business, Dynamic Adventures, she partners with executives, managers, and teams in Gulf Coast organizations to maximize performance in the workplace. She is an invited presenter and featured speaker for conferences and workshops across the United States. She received her master's and doctoral degrees from Louisiana State University. She is an avid reader, veteran traveler, and dedicated lifelong learner.

Index